Twelve Angry Men

A play

Reginald Rose

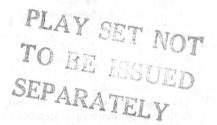

Samuel French — London
New York - Toronto - Hollywood

TWELVE ANGRY MEN

The Bristol Old Vic's new production, produced by Michael Edwards and Carole Winter, by arrangement with David Mirvish, opened at the Comedy Theatre, London, on 22nd April 1996, with the following cast:

Foreman	Stuart Rayner
2nd Juror	Kevin Dignam
3rd Juror	Tony Haygarth
4th Juror	Timothy West
5th Juror	Maurice Kaufmann
6th Juror	Douglas McFerran
7th Juror	Tim Healy
8th Juror	Kevin Whately
9th Juror	Alan MacNaughtan
10th Juror	Peter Vaughan
11th Juror	Robert East
12th Juror	Christopher Simon
Guard	Joshua Losey
Judge's voice	E. G. Marshall

Directed by Harold Pinter
Set designed by Eileen Diss
Costumes designed by Tom Rand
Lighting by Mick Hughes
Sound by Tom Lishman
Assistant Director Joe Harmston

TWELVE ANGRY MEN

Produced by Leo Genn and Kenneth Wagg at the Queen's
Theatre, London, on the 9th July 1964, with the following
cast of characters:

Guard	Eric Mason
Foreman of the Jury	Barry Lowe
Jurors	Olaf Pooley, Robert Urquhart, Walter Fitzgerald, Mark Kingston, John Bay, Ken Wayne, Leo Genn, Arnold Ridley, Grant Taylor, Peter Illing, Paul Maxwell
Voice of the Judge	James Dyrenforth

Directed by Margaret Webster
Setting by Norman Smith

CHARACTERS

1st Juror (Foreman)
2nd Juror
3rd Juror
4th Juror
5th Juror
6th Juror
7th Juror
8th Juror
9th Juror
10th Juror
11th Juror
12th Juror
Guard

Judge's Voice

Setting — The jury-room of a New York Court of Law
Time — 1957

ACT I

The jury-room of a New York Court of Law, 1957. A very hot summer afternoon

It is a large, drab, bare room in need of painting, with three windows in the back wall through which can be seen the New York skyline. Off the jury-room is a wash-room with wash-basin, soap and towels (visible on stage) and a lavatory beyond. A large, scarred table is centre with twelve chairs around it. A bench stands against the wall and there are several extra chairs and a small table in the room, plus a water-cooler, with paper cups and a waste-basket and an electric fan over the bench and a clock above the cooler and row of hooks for coats, with a shelf over it. There are pencils, pads and ashtrays on the table. At night the room is lit by fluorescent lighting with the switch next to the door

When the CURTAIN *rises, the room is empty. The voice of the judge is heard*

Judge's Voice ... and that concludes the court's explanation of the legal aspects of this case. And now, gentlemen of the jury, I come to my final instruction to you. Murder in the first degree — premeditated homicide — is the most serious charge tried in our criminal courts. You've listened to the testimony and you've had the law read to you and interpreted as it applies to this case. It now becomes your duty to try and separate the facts from the fancy. One man is dead. The life of another is at stake. I urge you to deliberate honestly and thoughtfully. If there is a reasonable doubt — then you must bring me a verdict of "not guilty". If, however, there is no reasonable doubt — then you must, in good conscience, find the accused guilty. However you decide, your verdict must be unanimous. In the event you find the accused guilty, the bench will not entertain a recommendation for mercy. The death sentence is mandatory in this case.

The door opens and the Guard enters. He carries a clipboard with a list of the jurors

I don't envy you your job. You are faced with a grave responsibility. Thank you, gentlemen.

There is a brief pause. Sound of Jurors walking, talking

Guard All right, let's move along, gentlemen.

The Jurors enter

The Guard checks his list

> *The 9th Juror, an old man, crosses, goes into the wash-room, and exits to the lavatory*

The 4th Juror begins to read a newspaper. Several Jurors open the windows. Others move awkwardly about the room. There is no conversation for a few moments. The 3rd Juror takes out some notes and studies them. The 2nd Juror crosses to the water-cooler, and gets a cup of water. The Foreman tears a sheet from a notepad and tears up little slips of paper for ballots. The Guard crosses to the 12th Juror and checks his name. The 7th Juror crosses to the 4th Juror and offers him a stick of gum. The 4th Juror shakes his head

7th Juror (*turning to the 8th Juror*) Do you want some gum?
8th Juror (*smiling*) No, thanks.

The 7th Juror vigorously chews a piece of gum himself and crosses to the 6th Juror

7th Juror (*mopping his brow*) Y'know something? I phoned up for the weather. This is the hottest day of the year.

The 6th Juror nods and gazes out of the window

You'd think they'd at least air-condition the place. I almost dropped dead in court.
Guard OK, gentlemen. Everybody's here. If there's anything you want, I'm right outside. Just knock.

The Guard exits and in the silence the sound is heard of the door being locked

5th Juror I never knew they locked the door.
10th Juror Sure they lock the door. What'd you think?
5th Juror I don't know. It just never occurred to me.

The 10th Juror crosses and pauses beside the Foreman and indicates the slips of paper

10th Juror Hey, what's that for?
Foreman Well, I figured we might want to vote by ballots.

10th Juror Great idea! Maybe we can get him elected senator. (*He laughs until he begins to cough*)

The Foreman looks at his watch and compares it with the clock. The 3rd Juror takes a cup of water from the water-cooler, moves to the 2nd Juror and looks around the room as he sips the water

3rd Juror (*to the 2nd Juror*) How'd you like it?
2nd Juror (*mildly*) I don't know, it was pretty interesting.
3rd Juror Yeah? I was falling asleep.
2nd Juror I mean, I've never been on a jury before.
3rd Juror Really? I've sat on juries, and it always amazes me the way these lawyers can talk, and talk and talk, even when the case is as obvious as this one. I mean, did you ever hear so much talk about nothing?
2nd Juror Well, I guess they're entitled.
3rd Juror Sure they are. Everybody deserves a fair trial. That's the system. Listen, I'm the last one to say anything against it, but I'm telling you sometimes I think we'd be better off if we took these tough kids and slapped 'em down before they make trouble, you know? Save us a lot of time and money.

The 2nd Juror looks nervously at the 3rd Juror, nods, rises, moves to the water-cooler, refills his cup and stands alone, sipping

7th Juror (*to the Foreman*) Hey, how about getting started here?
3rd Juror Yeah, let's get this over with. We've probably all got things to do.
Foreman Well, I was figuring we'd take a five-minute break. I mean, the old man's in the bathroom ...
5th Juror (*to the Foreman, hesitantly*) Are we going to sit in order?
Foreman I don't know.

The 8th Juror is looking out the window

12th Juror (*to the 8th Juror*) Not a bad view.

The 8th Juror nods

What d'you think of the case?

The 8th Juror doesn't answer

It had a lot of interest for me. No dead spots — know what I mean? I'll tell you we were lucky to get a murder case. I figured us for a burglary or an assault or something. Those can be the dullest. (*He looks out of the window*) Say, isn't that the Woolworth building?

8th Juror That's right.

12th Juror Funny, I've lived here all my life and I've never been in it.

The 8th Juror gazes out of the window. The 12th Juror looks at him for a moment then moves away

7th Juror (*to the10th Juror*) Goddamn waste of time. (*He laughs*)

10th Juror Yeah, can you imagine, sitting there for three days just for this?

7th Juror And what about that business with the knife? I mean, asking grown-up people to believe that kind of bullshit.

10th Juror Well, look, you've gotta expect that. You know what you're dealing with.

7th Juror Yeah, I suppose so.

The 10th Juror blows his nose vigorously

What's the matter, you got a cold?

10th Juror And how. These hot weather colds can kill you. I can hardly touch my nose. Know what I mean? (*He blows his nose loudly*)

7th Juror Well, your horn's all right. Now try your lights. (*He climbs on to the bench and tries the fan*) Oh, that's beautiful, the fan doesn't work. (*He steps down*) Somebody take a letter to the mayor. "Dear Stingy ... "

Foreman (*about the fan*) Let me take a look at it.

The 3rd Juror moves above the 4th Juror, leans over and scans the 4th Juror's newspaper. The Foreman climbs on the bench and examines the fan

It doesn't work. (*He climbs down*)

3rd Juror (*to the 4th Juror*) I didn't get a chance to look at the newspapers today. Anything new going on?

4th Juror I was just wondering how the market closed.

3rd Juror I wouldn't know. Say, are you on the Exchange or something?

4th Juror I'm a broker.

3rd Juror Really? I run a messenger service. "The Beck and Call Company." The name's my wife's idea. I employ thirty-seven people ... Started with nothing.

7th Juror (*looking at his watch*) Hey, Mr Foreman, let's go. What d'you say?

Foreman All right, gentlemen. Let's take seats.

7th Juror (*to the 2nd Juror*) This better be fast. I got tickets to a ball game tonight. Yankees—Cleveland. We got this new kid pitching, Modjelewski, or whatever his name is. He's a bull, this kid. (*He shoots his hand forward and out to indicate the path of a curve ball*) Shhooooom. A real jug handle.

There is no reaction at all from the 2nd Juror

You're quite a ball fan, aren't you?(*He turns to the Foreman*) Where do you want us to sit?

Foreman Well, I was thinking we ought to sit in order, by jury numbers. (*He points with each number*) Two, three, four, and so on, if that's OK with you gentlemen?

10th Juror What's the difference?

4th Juror I think it's reasonable to sit according to number.

10th Juror (*rising*) Let it be. (*He moves and sits on chair 10*)

The Jurors begin to take their seats. The 8th Juror continues to stare out of the window. The 9th Juror is still in the lavatory

12th Juror (*to the 11th Juror*) What was your impression of the prosecuting attorney?

11th Juror (*with a German accent*) I beg pardon?

12th Juror I thought he was really sharp. I mean, the way he hammered home his points, one by one, in logical sequence. It takes a good brain to do that. I was very impressed.

11th Juror Yes, I think he did an expert job.

12th Juror I mean, he had a lot of drive, too. Real drive.

7th Juror OK, let's get this show on the road.

Foreman (*to the 8th Juror*) How about sitting down?

The 8th Juror does not hear the Foreman

The gentleman at the window.

The 8th Juror turns, startled

How about sitting down?

8th Juror Oh, I'm sorry. (*He moves to his chair and sits*)

The 9th Juror enters the wash-room from the lavatory and washes his hands

10th Juror (*across the table to the 4th Juror*) It's pretty tough to figure, isn't it? A kid kills his father. Bing! Just like that.

12th Juror Well, if you analyse the figures ...

10th Juror What figures? It's those people! I'm tellin' you they let the kids run wild up there. Well, maybe it serves 'em right. Know what I mean?

The Foreman crosses to the wash-room door

7th Juror (*to the 5th Juror*) Hey, you a Yankee fan?
5th Juror No. Milwaukee.
7th Juror Milwaukee! That's like being hit on the head with a crowbar once a day. Listen, who they got — I'm asking you, who they got besides great groundskeepers?
Foreman (*to the 9th Juror*) We'd like to get started.

The 9th Juror enters from the wash-room

9th Juror I'm sorry.

The 9th Juror crosses and takes his seat

7th Juror Milwaukee!
Foreman All right. Now you gentlemen can handle this any way you want to. I mean, I'm not going to have any rules. If we want to discuss first and then vote, that's one way. Or we can vote right now to see how we stand. (*He pauses and looks around*) Well, that's all I have to say.
4th Juror I think it's customary to take a preliminary vote.
7th Juror Yeah, let's vote. Who knows, maybe we can all go home.
Foreman It's up to you. Just let's remember we've got a first degree murder charge here. If we vote "guilty", we send the accused to the electric chair. That's mandatory.
4th Juror I think we all know that.
3rd Juror Come on, let's vote.
10th Juror Yeah, let's see who's where.
Foreman Anybody doesn't want to vote? (*He looks around*)

The others are silent

All right. This has to be a twelve-to-nothing vote either way. That's the law. OK, are we ready? All those voting "guilty" raise your hands.

Seven or eight hands go up immediately. Several others go up more slowly. Everyone looks around the table as the Foreman rises and begins to count hands. The 9th Juror's hand goes up now, and all hands are raised except the 8th Juror's

... Nine — ten — eleven. That's eleven for "guilty". OK. "Not guilty"?

The 8th Juror slowly raises his hand

One. Right. OK, eleven to one — "guilty". Now we know where we are. (*He resumes his seat*)

10th Juror Boy-oh-boy! There's always one.

7th Juror (*after a pause*) So, what do we do now?

8th Juror Well, I guess we talk.

10th Juror Boy-oh-boy!

3rd Juror (*leaning over towards the 8th Juror*) Well, look, do you really think he's innocent?

8th Juror I don't know.

3rd Juror I mean, let's be reasonable. You sat in court and heard the same things we did. The man's a dangerous killer. You could see it.

8th Juror The man! He's sixteen years old.

3rd Juror Well, that's old enough. He knifed his own father. Four inches into the chest.

6th Juror (*to the 8th Juror*) It's pretty obvious. I mean, I was convinced from the first day.

3rd Juror Well, who wasn't? (*To the 8th Juror*) I really think this is one of those open and shut things. They proved it a dozen different ways. Would you like me to list them for you?

8th Juror No.

10th Juror Then what do you want?

8th Juror Nothing. I just want to talk.

7th Juror Well, what's there to talk about? Eleven men here agree. Nobody had to think twice about it, except you.

10th Juror I want to ask you something. Do you believe his story?

8th Juror I don't know whether I believe it or not. Maybe I don't.

7th Juror So what'd you vote "not guilty" for?

8th Juror There were eleven votes for "guilty". It's not easy for me to raise my hand and send a boy off to die without talking about it first.

7th Juror Who says it's easy for me?

8th Juror No-one.

7th Juror What, just because I voted fast? I think the guy's guilty. You couldn't change my mind if you talked for a hundred years.

8th Juror I'm not trying to change your mind. It's just that we're talking about somebody's life here. I mean, we can't decide in five minutes. Suppose we're wrong?

7th Juror Suppose we're wrong! Suppose this whole building fell on my head. You can suppose anything.

8th Juror That's right.

7th Juror (*after a pause*) What's the difference how long it takes? We honestly think he's guilty. So suppose we finish in five minutes? So what?

8th Juror Let's take an hour. The ball game doesn't start till eight o'clock.

7th Juror (*smiling*) OK, slugger, be my guest.

There is a silence

Foreman (*hesitantly*) Well, who's got something to say?

He looks at the 2nd Juror

How about you?

2nd Juror Not me.

9th Juror I'm willing to put in an hour.

10th Juror Great. I heard a pretty good story last night. This woman comes running into the doctor's office, stripped to the waist ——

8th Juror That's not what we're sitting here for.

10th Juror All right, then you tell me. What are we sitting here for?

8th Juror Maybe for no reason. I don't know. Look, this boy's been kicked around all his life. You know — living in a slum, his mother dead since he was nine. He spent a year and a half in an orphanage while his father served a jail term for forgery. That's not a very good head start. He's had a pretty terrible sixteen years. I think maybe we owe him a few words. That's all.

10th Juror I don't mind telling you this, mister. We don't owe him a thing. He got a fair trial, didn't he? What d'you think the trial cost? He's lucky he got it. Know what I mean? (*He rises and looks around at the others*) Look, we're all grown-ups here. We heard the facts, didn't we? Now, you're not going to tell us that we're supposed to believe that kid, knowing what he is. Listen, I've lived among 'em all my life. You can't believe a word they say. I mean, they're born liars.

9th Juror It suddenly occurs to me that you must be an ignorant man.

10th Juror What do you mean? What's he talking about?

9th Juror Do you think you have a monopoly on the truth?

10th Juror What are you making a Federal Case out of it for? (*To the others*) How d'ya like this guy?

9th Juror (*to the others*) I think certain things should be pointed out to this man.

3rd Juror All right. It's not Sunday. We don't need a sermon in here.

10th Juror Monopoly! For Chrissakes.

The 9th Juror half rises but then feels the 8th Juror's hand firmly on his arm, gently pulling him down. The 12th Juror doodles on his notepad

4th Juror If we're going to discuss this case, let's stick to the facts.

Foreman Right. We have a job to do. Let's do it. Maybe if the gentleman who's disagreeing down there could tell us why. You know, tell us what he thinks — we could show him where he's probably mixed up.

11th Juror (*looking at the 12th Juror's doodle*) What are you doing?

12th Juror Mmm? Oh. (*He holds up the doodle*) It's one of the products I work on at the ad agency. Rice Pops. "The Breakfast with the Built-in Bounce." I wrote that line.

11th Juror (*smiling in spite of himself*) It's very catchy.

Foreman If you don't mind!

The 2nd Juror rises, goes to the coat-hooks and takes a package of cough drops from his jacket pocket

12th Juror I'm sorry. I have this habit of doodling. It keeps me thinking clearly.

Foreman We're trying to get some place here. Y'know we can sit here forever ...

12th Juror Well, look, maybe this is an idea. I'm just thinking out loud, but it seems to me it's up to us to convince this gentleman — (*he indicates the 8th Juror*) that we're right and he's wrong. Maybe if we each took a minute or two. I mean, it's just a quick thought ...

Foreman No, I think it's a good one. Supposing we go once around the table in order of jury numbers.

7th Juror Anything. Let's start it off.

Foreman OK. (*To the 2nd Juror*) That means you're first.

2nd Juror Oh. Well ... (*He pauses nervously*) Well, it's hard to put into words. I just — think he's guilty. I thought it was obvious from the word go. I mean nobody proved otherwise.

8th Juror Nobody has to prove otherwise. The burden of proof is on the prosecution. The defendant doesn't have to open his mouth. That's in the Constitution. You've heard of it.

2nd Juror (*flustered*) Well, sure I've heard of it. I know what it is. I — what I meant — well, the man is guilty. I mean, somebody saw him do it. (*He looks around helplessly*)

3rd Juror OK. (*He refers to his notes*) Now, here's what I think, and I have no personal feelings about this. I'm talking facts. Number one. Let's take the old man who lived on the second floor right underneath the room where the murder took place. At ten minutes after twelve on the night of the killing he heard loud noises in the apartment upstairs. He said it sounded like a fight. Then he heard the kid shout out, "I'm gonna kill you." A second later he heard a body fall and he ran to the door of his apartment, looked out and saw the kid running down the stairs and out of the house. Then he called the police. They found the father with a knife in his chest.

Foreman And the coroner fixed the time of the death at around midnight.

3rd Juror Right. I mean, there are facts for you. You can't refute facts. This boy is guilty. Look, I'm as sentimental as the next guy. I know the kid is only sixteen, but he's still got to pay for what he did.

7th Juror I'm with you, pops.

4th Juror (*removing his eyeglasses*) It was obvious to me, anyway, that the boy's entire story was flimsy. He claimed he was at the movies during the time of the killing and yet one hour later he couldn't remember what films he saw or who played in them.

3rd Juror That's right. Did you hear that? (*To the 4th Juror*) You're absolutely right.

4th Juror No-one saw him going into or out of the theatre.

10th Juror Listen, what about that woman across the street? If her testimony don't prove it, nothing does.

11th Juror That's right. She was the one who actually saw the killing.

Foreman (*half rising*) Let's go in order here.

10th Juror (*rising, handkerchief in hand*) Just a minute. Here's a woman ... (*He blows his nose*) Here's a woman who's lying in bed and can't sleep. She's dying with the heat. Know what I mean? Anyway, she looks out the window and right across the street she sees the kid stick the knife into his father. The time is twelve ten on the nose. Everything fits. Look, she's known the kid all his life. His window is right opposite hers, across the el tracks, and she swore she saw him do it.

8th Juror Through the windows of a passing elevated train.

10th Juror Right. This el train had no passengers on it. It was just being moved downtown. The lights were out, remember? And they proved in court that at nights you can look through the windows of an el train when the lights are out and see what's happening on the other side. They proved it.

8th Juror (*to the 10th Juror*) I'd like to ask you something.

10th Juror Sure.

8th Juror You don't believe the boy. How come you believe the woman? She's one of "them", too, isn't she?

10th Juror (*suddenly angry*) You're a pretty smart fellow, aren't you?

The 10th Juror crosses towards the 8th Juror. Several jurors rise as if to intercept the 10th Juror

Foreman Hey, let's take it easy.

10th Juror (*angrily*) What's he so wise about? I'm telling you ...

3rd Juror Come on. Sit down. What are you letting him get you all upset for?

The 10th Juror sits

Foreman Let's calm down now. Let's try to keep it peaceful in here. Whose turn is it? (*To the 5th Juror*) OK. How about you?

5th Juror (*looking nervously around*) I'll pass it.

Foreman That's your privilege. How about the next gentleman?

6th Juror I don't know. I started to be convinced, uh — you know, very early in the case. Well, I was looking for the motive. That's very important. If there's no motive, where's the case? So anyway, that testimony from those people across the hall from the kid's apartment, that was very powerful. Didn't they say something about an argument between the father and the boy around seven o'clock that night? I mean, I can be wrong.

11th Juror It was eight o'clock. Not seven.

8th Juror That's right. Eight o'clock. They heard an argument, but they couldn't hear what it was about. Then they heard the father hit the boy twice, and finally they saw the boy walk angrily out of the house. What does that prove?

6th Juror Well, it doesn't exactly prove anything. It's just part of the picture. I didn't say it proved anything.

8th Juror You said it revealed a motive for the killing. The prosecuting attorney said the same thing. Well, I don't think it's a very strong motive. This boy has been hit so many times in his life that violence is practically a normal state of affairs for him. I can't see two slaps in the face provoking him into committing murder.

4th Juror (*quietly*) It may have been two slaps too many. Everyone has a breaking point.

Foreman (*to the 6th Juror*) Anything else?

6th Juror No.

Foreman OK. (*To the 7th Juror*) How about the next gentleman?

7th Juror Me? (*He pauses, looks around, shrugs*) I don't know, it's practically all said already. We can talk about it forever. I mean, this kid is oh for five. Look at his record. He was in Children's Court when he was ten for throwing a rock at his teacher. At fourteen he was in Reform School. He stole a car. He's been arrested for mugging. He was picked up twice for trying to slash another teenager with a knife. He's real quick with switch knives, they said. This is a very fine boy.

8th Juror Ever since he was five years old his father beat him up regularly. He used his fists.

7th Juror So would I. A kid like that.

4th Juror Wouldn't you call those beatings a motive for him to kill his father?

8th Juror (*after a pause*) I don't know. It's a motive for him to be an angry kid. I'll say that.

3rd Juror It's the kids, the way they are nowadays. Angry! Hostile! You can't do a damn thing with them. Just the way they talk to you. Listen, when I was his age I used to call my father "Sir". That's right, "Sir!" You ever hear a boy call his father that any more?

8th Juror Fathers don't seem to think it's important any more.

3rd Juror No? Have you got any kids?

8th Juror Two.

3rd Juror Yeah, well I've got one. He's twenty. We did everything for that boy and what happened? When he was nine he ran away from a fight. I saw him. I was so ashamed I almost threw up. So I told him right out. "I'm gonna make a man outa you or I'm gonna bust you in half trying." Well, I made a man outa him all right. When he was sixteen we had a battle. He hit me in the face. He's big, y'know. I haven't seen him in two years. Rotten kid. You work your heart out ... (*He breaks off. He has said more than he intended. He is embarrassed*) All right. Let's get on with it.

4th Juror (*rising*) I think we're missing the point here. This boy, let's say he's a product of a filthy neighbourhood and a broken home. We can't help that. We're here to decide whether he's guilty or innocent of murder, not to go into reasons why he grew up this way. He was born in a slum. Slums are breeding grounds for criminals. I know it. So do you. It's no secret. Children from slum backgrounds are potential menaces to society. Now I think ——

10th Juror (*interrupting*) Brother, you can say that again. The kids who crawl outa those places are real trash. I don't want any part of them, I'm telling you.

5th Juror (*rising*) I've lived in a slum all my life. I nurse that trash in Harlem Hospital six nights a week.

10th Juror Oh, now wait a second ...

5th Juror I used to play in a backyard that was filled with garbage. Maybe it still smells on me.

10th Juror (*his anger rising*) Now listen, buddy.

Foreman (*to the 5th Juror*) Now, let's be reasonable. There's nothing personal ...

5th Juror (*loudly*) There is something personal!

The 3rd Juror moves to the 5th Juror and pats him on the shoulder. The 5th Juror does not look up

3rd Juror Come on, now. He didn't mean you, feller. Let's not be so sensitive.

11th Juror This sensitivity I understand.

Foreman All right, let's stop all this arguing. We're wasting time here. (*He points to the 8th Juror*) It's your turn. Let's go.

8th Juror Well, I didn't expect a turn. I thought you were all supposed to be convincing me. Wasn't that the idea?

Foreman Check. I forgot that.

10th Juror Well, what's the difference? He's the one who's keeping us here. Let's hear what he's got to say.

Foreman Now just a second. We decided to do it a certain way. Let's stick to what we said.

10th Juror (*disgusted*) Ah, stop bein' a kid, will you?

Foreman A kid! Listen, what d'you mean by that?

10th Juror What d'ya think I mean? K-I-D, kid!

Foreman What, just because I'm trying to keep this thing organized? Listen. (*He rises*) You want to do it? Here. You sit here. You take the responsibility. I'll just shut up, that's all.

10th Juror Listen, what are you gettin' so hot about? Calm down, will ya?

Foreman Don't tell me to calm down. Here! Here's the chair. You keep it goin' smooth and everything. What d'ya think, it's a snap? Come on, Mr Foreman. Let's see how great you'd run the show.

10th Juror (*to the 11th Juror*) Did y'ever see such a thing?

Foreman You think it's funny or something?

12th Juror Take it easy. The whole thing's unimportant.

Foreman Unimportant? You want to try it?

12th Juror No. Listen, you're doing a beautiful job. Nobody wants to change.

7th Juror Yeah, you're doing great. Hang in there and pitch.

10th Juror All right. Let's hear from somebody.

There is a pause

8th Juror Well, if you want me to tell you how I feel about it right now, it's all right with me.

Foreman (*softly*) I don't care what you do.

8th Juror (*after a pause*) All right. I haven't got anything brilliant. I only know as much as you do. According to the testimony the boy looks guilty. Maybe he is. I sat there in court for three days listening while the evidence built up. Everybody sounded so positive that I started to get a peculiar feeling about this trial. I mean, nothing is that positive. I had questions I would have liked to ask. Maybe they wouldn't have meant anything. I don't know. But I started to feel that the defence counsel wasn't doing his job. He let too many things go. Little things.

10th Juror What little things? Listen, when these guys don't ask questions, that's because they know the answers already and they figure they'll be hurt.

8th Juror Maybe. It's also possible for a lawyer to be just plain stupid, isn't it?

6th Juror You sound like you've met my brother-in-law.

A few of the jurors laugh

8th Juror (*smiling*) I kept putting myself in the boy's place. I would have asked for another lawyer, I think. I mean, if I was on trial for my life I'd want my lawyer to tear the prosecution witnesses to shreds, or at least to try. Look, there was one alleged eyewitness to this killing. Someone else claims he heard the killing and then saw the boy running out afterwards. There was a lot of circumstantial evidence, but actually those two witnesses were the entire case for the prosecution. Supposing they were wrong?

12th Juror What do you mean, "Supposing they were wrong?" What's the point of having witnesses at all?

8th Juror Could they be wrong?

12th Juror They sat on the stand under oath. What are you trying to say?

8th Juror They're only people. People make mistakes. Could they be wrong?

12th Juror I ... No! I don't think so.

8th Juror Do you know so?

12th Juror Well, now, listen. Nobody can know a thing like that. This isn't an exact science.

8th Juror That's right. It isn't.

3th Juror (*rising angrily*) All right. (*To the 8th Juror*) Let's try to get to the point here. What about the switch-knife they found in the father's chest?

2nd Juror Well, wait a minute. I think we oughta ... There are some people who haven't talked yet. Shouldn't we ... ?

3rd Juror Look, they can talk whenever they like. Now just be quiet a second, will you? (*He turns to the 8th Juror*) OK, what about the knife? You know, the one that fine, upright boy admitted buying on the night of the murder. Let's talk about that.

8th Juror All right, let's talk about it. Let's get it in here and look at it. I'd like to see it again. (*He turns to the Foreman*) Mr Foreman?

The Foreman rises and crosses to the door

3rd Juror We all know what it looks like.

The Foreman knocks on the door

The Guard unlocks the door and enters

The Foreman whispers to him

  The Guard nods and exits, locking the door

What are we gonna get out of seeing it again?

5th Juror You brought it up.

4th Juror The gentleman has a right to see exhibits in evidence. (*To the 8th Juror*) The knife, and the way it was bought, is pretty strong evidence. Don't you think so?

8th Juror I do.

4th Juror Good. Now suppose we take these facts one at a time. One. The boy admitted going out of his house at eight o'clock on the night of the murder after being punched several times by his father.

8th Juror He didn't say "punched". He said "hit." There's a difference between a slap and a punch.

4th Juror After being hit several times by his father. Two. The boy went directly to a neighbourhood junk shop where he bought a ... What do you call these things —

3rd Juror } (*together*) { Switch-knives.
4th Juror }   { — a switch-blade knife. (*To the 3rd Juror*) Thank you.

4th Juror Three. This wasn't what you'd call an ordinary knife. It had a very unusual carved handle. Four. The storekeeper who sold it to him identified the knife in court and said it was the only one of its kind he had ever had in stock. Five. At, oh, about eight forty-five the boy ran into three friends of his in front of a diner. Am I correct so far?

8th Juror Yes, you are.

3rd Juror (*to the 8th Juror*) You bet he is. (*To the others*) Now, listen to this man. He knows what he's talking about.

4th Juror The boy talked with his friends for about an hour, leaving them at nine forty-five. During this time they saw the switch-knife. Six. Each of them identified the death weapon in court as that same knife. Seven. The boy arrived home at about ten o'clock. Now this is where the stories offered by the boy and the State begin to diverge slightly. He claims that he stayed home until eleven thirty and then went to one of those all-night movies. He returned home at about three fifteen in the morning to find his father dead and himself arrested. Now, what happened to the switch-knife? This is the charming and imaginative little fable the boy invented. He claims that the knife fell through a hole in his pocket some time between eleven thirty and three fifteen while he was on his trip to the movies and that he never saw it again. Now this is a tale, gentlemen. I think it's quite clear that the boy never went to the movies that night. No-one in the house saw him go out at eleven thirty. No-one at the theatre identified him. He couldn't even remember the names of the pictures he saw. What actually happened is this: the boy stayed home, had another fight with this father, stabbed him to death with the knife at ten minutes after twelve and fled from the house. He even remembered to wipe the knife clean of fingerprints.

The Guard unlocks the door and enters carrying a curiously designed knife with a tag hanging from it

The 4th Juror goes to the Guard, and takes the knife from him

The Guard exits and locks the door

Everyone connected with the case identified the knife. Now are you trying to tell me that it really fell through a hole in the boy's pocket and that someone picked it up off the street, went to the boy's house and stabbed his father with it just to be amusing?

8th Juror No. I'm saying it's possible that the boy lost the knife and that someone else stabbed his father with a similar knife. It's possible.

The 4th Juror flicks open the knife and jams it into the table

4th Juror Take a look at that knife. I've never seen one like it. Neither had the storekeeper who sold it to the boy. Aren't you asking us to accept a pretty incredible coincidence?

8th Juror I'm not asking anyone to accept it. I'm just saying that it's possible.

3rd Juror (*shouting*) And I'm saying it's not possible.

The 8th Juror stands for a moment in silence, then he reaches into his pocket and swiftly withdraws a knife. He holds it in front of his face and flicks open the blade, then he leans forward and sticks the knife into the table alongside the other. They are exactly alike. There is a burst of sound in the room. The 8th Juror stands back from the table, watching

6th Juror Look at it! It's the same knife.

7th Juror What is this?

12th Juror Where'd that come from?

2nd Juror How d'you like that?

3rd Juror (*looking at the 8th Juror; amazed*) What are you trying to do?

10th Juror Yeah. What's going on here? Who do you think you are?

4th Juror Quiet! Let's be quiet. (*To the 8th Juror*) Where d'you get that knife?

8th Juror I was walking for a couple of hours last·night, just thinking. I walked through the boy's neighbourhood. The knife comes from a little pawnshop three blocks from his house. It cost six dollars.

4th Juror It's against the law to buy or sell switch-blade knives.

8th Juror That's right. I broke the law.

3rd Juror Listen. You pulled a real bright trick here. Now, supposing you tell me what you proved. Maybe there are ten knives like that. So what?

8th Juror Maybe there are.

3rd Juror So what does that mean? It's the same kind of knife. So what's that? The discovery of the age or something?

11th Juror It would still be an incredible coincidence for another person to have stabbed the father with the same kind of knife.

3rd Juror That's right! He's right.

7th Juror The odds are a million to one.

8th Juror It's possible.

4th Juror But not very probable.

Foreman Listen, let's take seats. There's no point in milling round here.

They begin to move back to their seats. The 8th Juror stands watching

2nd Juror It's interesting that he'd find a knife exactly like the one the boy bought.

3rd Juror What's interesting? You think it proves anything?

2nd Juror Well, no. I was just ——

3rd Juror Interesting! (*He points at the 8th Juror*) Listen, how come the kid bought the knife to begin with?

8th Juror Well, he claims that ——

3rd Juror I know. He claims he bought it as a present for a friend of his. He was gonna give it to him the next day because he busted the other kid's knife dropping it on the pavement.

8th Juror That's what he said.

7th Juror Baloney!

9th Juror The friend testified that the boy did break his knife.

3rd Juror Yeah. And how long before the killing? Three weeks. Right? So how come our noble lad bought this knife one half-hour after his father smacked him and three and a half hours before they found it shoved up here in the father's chest?

7th Juror Well, he was gonna give the knife to his friend. He just wanted to use it for a minute.

There is scattered laughter

8th Juror (*to the 3rd Juror*) Let me ask you this. It's one of the questions I wanted to ask in court. If the boy bought the knife to use on his father, how come he showed what was going to be the murder weapon to three friends of his just a couple of hours before the killing?

3rd Juror Listen, all of this is just talk. The boy lied and you know it.

8th Juror He may have lied. (*To the 10th Juror*) Do you think he lied?

10th Juror Now that's a stupid question. Sure he lied.

8th Juror (*to the 4th Juror*) Do you?

4th Juror You know my answer. He lied.

8th Juror (*to the 5th Juror*) Do you think he lied?

5th Juror I'm not sure ... (*He breaks off and looks nervously around*)

3rd Juror (*leaping into the breach*) You're not sure about what? Now wait a second. (*To the 8th Juror*) What are you, the kid's lawyer or something? Who do you think you are to start cross-examining us?

8th Juror Isn't that what's supposed to happen in a jury-room?

3rd Juror Listen, there are still eleven of us in here who think he's guilty.

7th Juror Yeah. What do you think you're gonna accomplish? You're not gonna change anybody's mind. So if you want to be stubborn and hang this jury, go ahead. The kid'll be tried again and found guilty sure as he's born.

8th Juror You're probably right.

7th Juror So what are you gonna do about it? We can be here all night.

9th Juror It's only one night. A boy may die.

7th Juror Brother! Anybody got a deck of cards?

2nd Juror (*to the Foreman*) I don't think he ought to make a joke about it.

Foreman What do you want me to do?

10th Juror Listen, I don't see what all this stuff about the knife has to do with anything. Somebody saw the kid stab his father. What more do we need? I got three garages of mine going to pot while you're talking. Let's get done and get outa here.

11th Juror The knife was very important to the district attorney. He spent one whole morning ...

10th Juror He's a fifteenth assistant, or something. What does he know?

Foreman OK. I think we oughta get on with it now. These side arguments only slow us up. (*To the 8th Juror*) What about it?

6th Juror (*to the 8th Juror*) You're the only one.

8th Juror I have a proposition to make to all of you. I want to call for a vote. I'd like you eleven men to vote by secret written ballot. I'll abstain. If there are still eleven votes for guilty, I won't stand alone. We'll take a guilty verdict in to the judge right now. But if anyone votes not guilty, we'll stay and talk this thing out. (*He pauses*) Well, that's all. If you want to try it, I'm ready.

3rd Juror Well, finally you're behaving like a reasonable man.

12th Juror Check. I'll buy that.

7th Juror OK. Let's do it.

Foreman That sounds fair.

Some of the Jurors nod. The 8th Juror moves to the window

Anyone doesn't agree? OK. Pass these along. (*He passes out slips of paper*)

The 8th Juror stands watching the others. The jurors pass the slips along. Finally each of them begins to write. Now some of them begin to fold their slips and pass them back to the Foreman. The Foreman stacks all the slips on the table in front of him. He picks up the first slip of paper, opens it and reads

"Guilty."

He opens and reads the other slips in turn

"Guilty." "Guilty." "Guilty." "Guilty." "Guilty." "Guilty." "Guilty." "Guilty." "Not Guilty."

There is a babble of voices. The 8th Juror relaxes, moves to his chair and sits

(*Reading the last slip*) "Guilty."
10th Juror Boy! How do you like that?
7th Juror And another chap flips his goddamn wig!
10th Juror All right, who was it? Come on. I want to know.
11th Juror Excuse me. This was a secret ballot. We agreed on this.
3rd Juror Secret? What d'ya mean, secret? There are no secrets in a jury-room. I know who it was. (*He crosses to the 5th Juror*) Brother, you're really something! You come in here and you vote guilty like everybody else, and then this golden-voiced preacher over here starts to tear your heart out with stories about a poor little kid who just couldn't help becoming a murderer. So you change your vote. If that isn't the most sickening ... Why don'tcha drop a quarter in his collection box?
5th Juror Now wait a minute.

The 3rd Juror turns away

You can't talk to me like that!

The 3rd Juror turns to face him. The 4th Juror slips in between them and takes the 5th Juror by the arm

No. (*He shakes off the 4th Juror*) Where does he get the right to shout at me?
4th Juror All right, let's calm down.

5th Juror Who does he think he is? I mean, did you see him?

4th Juror Just sit down. He's very excitable. Forget it. It doesn't matter.

3rd Juror You bet I'm excitable. We're trying to put a guilty man into the chair where he belongs and all of a sudden somebody's telling us fairy tales — and we're listening.

2nd Juror (*mildly*) Take it easy.

3rd Juror What do you mean — take it easy! D'you feel like seeing a proven murderer walking the streets? Why don't we give him his knife back? Make it easier for him.

Foreman OK, let's stop the yelling. Who's got something constructive to say?

11th Juror Please. I would like to say something here. I have always thought that in this country a man was entitled to have unpopular opinions ...

7th Juror Let's stick to the subject. (*To the 5th Juror*) What made you change your vote?

9th Juror He didn't change his vote. I did. Would you like me to tell you why?

7th Juror No, I wouldn't like you to tell me why.

9th Juror Well, I'd like to make it clear, anyway, if you don't mind.

10th Juror Do we have to listen to this?

6th Juror Hey, look! The man wants to talk.

9th Juror Thank you. (*To the 7th Juror*) This gentleman — (*he indicates the 8th Juror*) has been standing alone against us. He doesn't say the boy is not guilty. He just isn't sure. Well, it's not easy to stand alone against the ridicule of others. He gambled for support and I gave it to him. I respect his motives. The boy on trial is probably guilty. But I want to hear more.

The 7th Juror crosses to the wash-room

For the time being the vote is ten to two.

The 7th Juror enters the wash-room, slams the door after him

I'm talking here. You have no right to ...

8th Juror (*to the 9th Juror*) He can't hear you. He never will.

3rd Juror Well, if the speech is over, maybe we can go on.

Foreman I think we ought to take a break. One man's inside there. Let's wait for him.

The Foreman moves above the table to where the two knives are stuck into it. He plucks the tagged knife out and closes it

12th Juror (*to the 11th Juror*) Looks like we're really hung up here. I mean, that thing with the old man was pretty unexpected. I wish I knew how we could break this up. (*He smiles suddenly*) Y'know, in advertising ... I told you I worked at an ad agency, didn't I?

The Foreman crosses to the door and knocks

The Guard unlocks the door and enters

The Foreman hands him the knife

The Guard exits, locking the door

Well, there are some pretty strange people — not strange, really — they just have peculiar ways of expressing themselves, y'know what I mean?

The 11th Juror nods

Well, it's probably the same in your business — right? What do you do?
11th Juror I'm a watchmaker.
12th Juror Really? The finest watchmakers come from Europe, I imagine.

The 11th Juror bows slightly

The 6th Juror rises, and goes into the lavatory

Anyway, I was telling you — in the agency, when they reach a point like this in a meeting, there's always some character ready with an idea. And it kills me, I mean it's the weirdest thing sometimes the way they precede the idea with some kind of phrase. Like — oh, some account exec'll say, "Here's an idea. Let's run it up the flagpole and see if anyone salutes it," or "Put it on a bus and see if it gets off at Wall Street." I mean, it's idiotic, but it's funny.

The 8th Juror goes into the wash-room and hangs his jacket on a hook. The 3rd Juror crosses to the 5th Juror

3rd Juror (*to the 5th Juror*) Look, I was a little excited. Well, you know how it is — I didn't mean to get nasty or anything.

The 5th Juror crosses away from the 3rd Juror without answering. The 7th Juror steps away from the wash-basin and dries his hands. The 8th Juror crosses to the wash-basin

7th Juror (*to the 8th Juror*) Say, are you a salesman?

8th Juror I'm an architect.

7th Juror You know what the soft sell is? You're pretty good at it. I'll tell ya. I got a different technique. Jokes. Drinks. Knock 'em on their asses. I made twenty-seven thousand last year selling marmalade. That's not bad. Considering marmalade. (*He watches the 8th Juror for a moment*) What are ya getting out of it — kicks? The boy is guilty, pal. So let's go home before we get sore throats.

8th Juror What's the difference whether you get one here or at the ball game?

7th Juror No difference pal. No difference at all.

The 7th Juror goes back into the jury-room

The 6th Juror enters from the lavatory, goes to the wash-basin and washes his hands

6th Juror (*to the 8th Juror*) Nice bunch of guys.

8th Juror I guess they're the same as any.

6th Juror That loud, heavy-set guy, the one who was tellin' us about his kid — the way he was talking — boy, that was an embarrassing thing.

8th Juror Yeah.

6th Juror What a murderous day. You think we'll be here much longer.

8th Juror I don't know.

6th Juror He's guilty for sure. There's not a doubt in the whole world. We shoulda been done already. Listen, I don't care, y'know. It beats workin'.

The 8th Juror smiles

You think he's innocent?

8th Juror I don't know. It's possible.

6th Juror I don't know you, but I'm bettin' you've never been wronger in your life. Y'oughta wrap it up. You're wastin' your time.

8th Juror Suppose you were the one on trial?

6th Juror I'm not used to supposing. I'm just a working man. My boss does the supposing. But I'll try one. Suppose you talk us all outa this and the kid really did knife his father?

The 6th Juror looks at the 8th Juror for a moment, then goes into the jury-room. The 8th Juror stands alone for a few moments and we know that this is the problem which has been tormenting him. He does not know, and never will. He switches out the wash-room light and goes into the jury-room

Foreman OK, let's take seats.

2nd Juror Looks like we'll be here for dinner.

Foreman OK. Let's get down to business. Who wants to start it off?

There is a pause, then the 4th and 6th Jurors start to speak at the same time

6th Juror ⎫
                    ⎰ *(together)* ⎰ Well, I'd like to make a point. (*To the 4th Juror*)
                    ⎱   ⎱ Pardon me.
4th Juror ⎭   Maybe it would be profitable if we ... (*To the 6th
                                     Juror*) I'm sorry, go ahead.

6th Juror I didn't mean to interrupt.

4th Juror No. Go ahead. It's all right.

6th Juror Well. I was going to say, well, this is probably a small point, but
anyway ... (*to the 8th Juror*) The boy had a motive for the killing. You
know, the beatings and all. So if he didn't do it, who did? Who else had the
motive? That's my point. I mean, nobody goes out and kills someone
without a motive, not unless he's just plain nuts. Right?

8th Juror As far as I know, we're supposed to decide whether or not the boy
on trial is guilty beyond a reasonable doubt. We're not concerned with
anyone else's motives here. That's a job for the police.

4th Juror Very true. But we can't help letting the only motive we know of
creep into our thoughts, can we? And we can't help asking ourselves who
else might have had a motive. Logically, these things follow. (*He nods
towards the 6th Juror*) This gentleman is asking a reasonable question.
Somebody killed him. If it wasn't the boy, who was it?

3rd Juror Modjelewski.

7th Juror You're talking about the man I love!

4th Juror If you haven't got anything to add besides jokes, I suggest you
listen.

3rd Juror OK. It's just letting off steam. I'm sorry. Go ahead.

4th Juror (*to the 8th Juror*) Well, maybe you can answer me. Who else
might have killed the father?

8th Juror Well, I don't know. The father wasn't exactly a model citizen. The
boy's lawyer outlined his background in his closing statement. He was in
prison once. He was known to be a compulsive gambler and a pretty
consistent loser. He spent a lot of time in neighbourhood bars and he'd get
into fist fights sometimes after a couple of drinks. Usually over a woman.
He was a tough, cruel, primitive kind of man who never held a job for more
than six months in his life. So here are a few possibilities. He could have
been murdered by one of many men he served time with in prison. By a
bookmaker. By a man he'd beaten up. By a woman he'd picked up. By any
one of the people he was known to hang out with.

10th Juror Boy-oh-boy, that's the biggest load of crap I ever ... Listen, we know the father was a bum. So what has that got to do with anything?

8th Juror I didn't bring it up. I was asked who else might have killed him. I gave my answer.

9th Juror (*pointing at the 4th Juror*) That gentleman over there asked a direct question.

10th Juror Everyone's a lawyer!

3rd Juror Look, suppose you answer this for me. The old man who lived downstairs heard the kid yell out, "I'm going to kill you." A split second later he heard a body hit the floor. Then he saw the kid run out of the house. Now what does all that mean to you?

8th Juror I was wondering how clearly the old man could have heard the boy's voice through the ceiling.

3rd Juror He didn't hear it through the ceiling. His window was open and so was the window upstairs. It was a hot night, remember?

8th Juror The voice came from another apartment. It's not easy to identify a voice, especially a shouting voice.

Foreman He identified it in court. He picked the boy's voice out of five other voices, blindfolded.

8th Juror That was just an ambitious district attorney putting on a show. Look, the old man knows the boy's voice very well. They've lived in the same house for years. But to identify it positively from the apartment downstairs ... Isn't it possible he was wrong — that maybe he thought the boy was upstairs and automatically decided that the voice he heard was the boy's voice?

4th Juror I think that's a bit far-fetched.

10th Juror Brother, you can say that again. (*To the 8th Juror*) Look. The old man heard the father's body falling and then he saw the boy run out of the house fifteen seconds later. He saw the boy.

12th Juror Check. And don't forget the woman across the street. She looked right into the open window and saw the boy stab his father. I mean, isn't that enough for you?

8th Juror Not right now. No, it isn't.

7th Juror How do you like him? It's like talking into a dead phone.

4th Juror The woman saw the killing through the windows of a moving elevated train. The train had six cars and she saw it through the windows of the last two cars. She remembered the most insignificant details. I don't see how you can argue with that.

3rd Juror (*to the 8th Juror*) Well, what have you got to say about it?

8th Juror I don't know. It doesn't sound right to me.

3rd Juror Well, suppose you think about it. (*To the 12th Juror*) Lend me your pencil.

The12th Juror hands the pencil to the 3rd Juror who starts to draw what is obviously a tic-tac-toe pattern on the pad. (See note on Page 59)

8th Juror I wonder if anybody has any idea how long it takes an elevated train ...

The 8th Juror sees the 3rd Juror and the 12th Juror playing tic-tac-toe, snatches up the pad, tears off the top sheet, crumples it and drops it in the waste-basket

3rd Juror Wait a minute!

8th Juror This isn't a game.

3rd Juror (*shouting*) Who do you think you are?

12th Juror (*to the 3rd Juror*) All right, take it easy.

Foreman Come on now, sit down.

3rd Juror I've got a good mind to belt him one.

Foreman Now, please! I don't want any fights in here.

3rd Juror Did you see him? The nerve! The absolute nerve!

10th Juror All right. Forget it. It's not important. Know what I mean?

3rd Juror "This isn't a game." Who does he think he's dealing with here?

Foreman Come on, now. It's all over. Let's take our seats.

3rd Juror What's all over? I want an apology.

6th Juror OK, noisy. He apologizes. Now let's hear what the man has to say.

8th Juror Thank you. I wonder if anybody has an idea how long it takes an elevated train going at medium speed to pass a given point?

7th Juror What has that got to do with anything?

8th Juror How long? Take a guess.

4th Juror I wouldn't have the slightest idea.

8th Juror (*to the 5th Juror*) What do you think?

5th Juror I don't know. About ten or twelve seconds, maybe.

3rd Juror What's all this for?

8th Juror I'd say that was a fair guess. Anyone else?

11th Juror That sounds right to me.

10th Juror Come on, what's the guessing game for?

8th Juror (*to the 2nd Juror*) What would you say?

2nd Juror Ten seconds. Approximately.

4th Juror All right. Say ten seconds. What are you getting at?

8th Juror This. It takes a six-car el train ten seconds to pass a given point. Now say that given point is the open window of the room in which the killing took place. You can almost reach out the window of that room and touch the el tracks. Right?

5th Juror Right.

8th Juror All right. Now let me ask you this — has anyone here ever lived right next to the el tracks?

6th Juror Well, I just finished painting an apartment that overlooked an el line. I'm a house painter, y'know. I was there for three days.

8th Juror What was it like?

6th Juror What d'ya mean?

8th Juror Noisy?

6th Juror Brother! Well, it didn't matter. We're all punchy in our business, anyway. (*He laughs*)

8th Juror I lived in a second-floor apartment next to an el line once. When the window's open and the train goes by, the noise is almost unbearable. You can't hear yourself think.

3rd Juror OK. You can't hear yourself think. Will you get to the point?

8th Juror I will. Let's take two pieces of testimony and try to put them together. First, the old man in the apartment downstairs. He says he heard the boy say, "I'm going to kill you" and a split second later he heard the body hit the floor. One second later. Right?

2nd Juror That's right.

8th Juror Second, the woman in the apartment across the street. She claimed that she looked out of her window and saw the killing through the last two cars of a passing elevated train. Right? The last two cars.

3rd Juror All right. What point are you making here?

8th Juror Now, we agreed that an el train takes about ten seconds to pass a given point. Since the woman saw the stabbing through the last two cars we can assume that the body fell to the floor just as the train passed by. Therefore, the el train had been roaring by the old man's window for a full ten seconds before the body fell. The old man, according to his own testimony, hearing "I'm going to kill you" and the body falling a split second later, would have had to hear the boy make this statement while the el was roaring past his nose. It's not possible that he could have heard it.

3rd Juror That's idiotic! Sure he could have heard it.

8th Juror (*to the 3rd Juror*) Do you think so?

3rd Juror The old man said the boy yelled it out. That's enough for me.

8th Juror If he heard anything at all, he still couldn't have identified the voice with the el roaring by.

3rd Juror You're talking about a matter of seconds here. Nobody can be that accurate.

8th Juror Well, I think that testimony which could put a human being into the electric chair should be that accurate.

5th Juror I don't think he could have heard it.

6th Juror Yeah. Maybe he didn't hear it. I mean, with the el noise ...

3rd Juror What are you people talking about?

5th Juror Well, it stands to reason ...

3rd Juror You're crazy! Why should he lie? What's he got to gain?

9th Juror Attention, maybe.

3rd Juror You keep coming up with these bright sayings. Why don't you send one in to a newspaper? They pay three dollars.

6th Juror (*to the 3rd Juror*) Hey! What're ya talking to him like that for?

The 3rd Juror looks at the 6th Juror, then turns disgustedly away. The 6th Juror reaches out and turns the 3rd Juror firmly around by the arm

A guy who talks like that to an old man oughta really get stepped on y'know.

3rd Juror Get your hands off me!

6th Juror You oughta have some respect, mister. If you say stuff like that to him again — I'm gonna lay you out.

The 6th Juror releases the 3rd Juror and speaks to the 9th Juror

Go ahead. You can say anything you want. Why do you think the old man might lie?

9th Juror It's just that I looked at him for a very long time. The seam of his jacket was split under his arm. Did you notice it? I mean, to come into court like that. He was a very old man with a torn jacket and he walked very slowly to the stand. He was dragging his left leg and trying to hide it because he was ashamed. I think I know him better than anyone here. This is a quiet, frightened, insignificant old man who has been nothing all his life, who has never had recognition, his name in the newspapers. Nobody knows him, nobody quotes him, nobody seeks his advice after seventy-five years. That's a very sad thing, to be nothing. A man like this needs to be recognized, to be listened to, to be quoted just once. This is very important. It would be so hard for him to recede into the background ...

7th Juror Now, wait a minute. Are you trying to tell us he'd lie just so that he could be important once?

9th Juror No. He wouldn't really lie. But perhaps he'd make himself believe that he'd heard those words and recognized the boy's face.

10th Juror Well, that's the most fantastic story I've ever heard. How can you make up a thing like that? What do you know about it?

The 9th Juror lowers his head, embarrassed

4th Juror Gentlemen, this case is based on a reasonable and logical progression of facts. Let's keep it there.

11th Juror Facts may be coloured by the personalities of the people who present them.

2nd Juror Anybody want a cough drop?
10th Juror I'll take one.

The 2nd Juror offers the cough drops to the 10th Juror. The10th Juror takes one

Thanks.

12th Juror Say what you like, I still don't see how anybody can think the boy's not guilty.

8th Juror There's another thing I wanted to talk about for a minute. I think we've proved that the old man couldn't have heard the boy say, "I'm going to kill you", but supposing ——

10th Juror You didn't prove it at all. What are you talking about?

8th Juror But supposing he really did hear it. This phrase, how many times has each of us used it? Probably hundreds. "I could kill you for that, darling." "If you do that once more, Junior, I'm going to kill you." "Come on, Rocky, kill him." We say it every day. It doesn't mean we're going to kill someone.

3rd Juror Wait a minute! What are you trying to give us here? The phrase was, "I'm going to kill you," and the kid screamed it out at the top of his lungs. Don't tell me he didn't mean it. Anybody says a thing like that the way he said it, they mean it.

2nd Juror Well, gee, I don't know. I remember I was arguing with the guy I work next to at the bank a couple of weeks ago; so he called me an idiot; so I yelled at him ...

3rd Juror No listen, this guy is making you believe things that aren't so. The kid said he was going to kill him and he did kill him.

8th Juror Well, let me ask you this: do you really think the boy would shout out a thing like that so the whole neighbourhood would hear it? I don't think so. He's much too bright for that.

10th Juror Bright? He's a common, ignorant slob. He don't even speak good English.

11th Juror He doesn't even speak good English.

5th Juror I'd like to change my vote to "not guilty".

7th Juror Now you've got to be kidding.

5th Juror You heard.

Foreman Are you sure?

5th Juror Yes, I'm sure.

Foreman The vote is nine to three in favour of "guilty".

7th Juror Well, if that isn't the livin' end! What are you basing it on? Stories this guy made up. He oughta write for *Amazing Detective Monthly*. He'd make a fortune. (*To the 5th Juror*) Listen, there are facts staring you right in your face. Every one of them says this kid killed his old man. For cryin' out loud, his own lawyer knew he didn't stand a chance right from the beginning. His own lawyer. You could see it. He deserves the chair.

8th Juror Does he? It's happened before that someone's been convicted of murder and executed, and years later someone else has confessed to the crime. Sometimes ... Sometimes the facts that are staring you in the face are wrong!

7th Juror (*to the 8th Juror*) I'm talkin' to him — (*he indicates the 5th Juror*) not to you. (*To the others*) Boy, this guy is really something. (*To the 8th Juror*) Listen, the kid had a lawyer, didn't he? The lawyer presented his case, not you. How come you've got so much to say?

8th Juror The lawyer was court-appointed.

7th Juror So what does that mean?

8th Juror Well, it could mean a lot of things. It could mean he didn't want the case. It could mean he resented being appointed. It's the kind of case that brings him nothing. No money. No glory. Not even much chance of winning. It's not a very promising situation for a young lawyer. He'd really have to believe in his client to make a good fight. As you pointed out a minute ago, he obviously didn't.

7th Juror Sure he didn't. Who in hell could, except God come to earth or somebody? (*He looks at his watch then up at the clock*) Come on already! Look at the time!

11th Juror Pardon me, but I have made some notes here.

10th Juror Notes yet!

11th Juror I would like please to say something. I have been listening very closely, and it seems to me that this man — (*he indicates the 8th Juror*) has some very good points to make. From what was presented at the trial the boy looks guilty, but maybe if we go deeper ——

10th Juror Come on, will ya?

11th Juror There is a question I would like to ask. We assume that the boy committed murder. He stabbed his father in the chest and ran away. This was at ten minutes after twelve. Now, how was he caught by the police? He came home at three o'clock or so and was captured by two detectives in the hallway of his house. My question is, if he really had killed his father, why would he come back three hours later? Wouldn't he be afraid of being caught?

3rd Juror Look — he came home to get his knife. It's not nice to leave knives sticking around in people's chests.

7th Juror Yeah, especially relatives'.

4th Juror (*to the 11th Juror*) The boy knew that there were people who could identify the knife as the one he had just bought. He had to get it before the police did.

11th Juror But if he knew the knife could be identified, why did he leave it there in the first place?

4th Juror Well, I think we can assume he ran out in a state of panic after he killed his father, and then when he finally calmed down, he realized that he had left the knife there.

11th Juror This then depends on your definition of panic. He was calm enough to see to it that there were no fingerprints on the knife. Now where did his panic start and where did it end?

3rd Juror Look, you can forget all that other stuff. He still came home to dig out his knife and get rid of it.

11th Juror Three hours later?

3rd Juror Sure, three hours later.

11th Juror If I were the boy and I had killed my father, I would not have come home three hours later. I would be afraid that the police would be there. I would stay away, knife or no knife.

3rd Juror Listen, you voted "guilty", didn't you? What side are you on?

11th Juror I don't believe I have to be loyal to one side or the other. I am simply asking questions.

12th Juror Well, this is just off the top of my head, but if I were the boy, and I'd, you know, done the stabbing and everything, I'd take a chance and go back for the knife. I'll bet he figured no-one had seen him and that the body probably wasn't even discovered yet. After all, it was the middle of the night. He probably thought no-one would find the body till the next day.

11th Juror Pardon. Here is my whole point. The woman across the street testified that a moment after she saw the killing, that is, a moment after the el train went by, she screamed and then went to telephone the police. Now, the boy must certainly have heard that scream and known that somebody saw something. I don't think he would have gone back if he had been the murderer.

4th Juror Two points. One: in his state of panic he may not have heard the scream. Perhaps it wasn't very loud. Two: if he did hear it, he may not have connected it with his own act. Remember, he lived in a neighbourhood where screams were fairly commonplace.

3rd Juror Right! There's your answer.

8th Juror Maybe. Maybe he did stab his father, didn't hear the woman's screams, did run out in a panic, did calm down three hours later and came back to try and get the knife, risking being caught by the police. Maybe all those things are so. But maybe they're not. I think there's enough doubt to make us wonder whether he was there at all during the time the murder took place.

10th Juror What d'ya mean doubt? What are you talking about? Didn't the old man see him running out of the house? He's twisting the facts. I'm telling you! (*To the 11th Juror*) Did or didn't the old man see the kid running out of the house at twelve ten? Well, did he or didn't he?

11th Juror He says he did.

10th Juror Says he did! (*To the others*) Boy-oh-boy! How do you like that? (*To the 11th Juror*) Well, did or didn't the woman across the street see the kid kill his father? She says she did. You're makin' out like it don't matter what people say. What you want to believe, you believe, and what you don't want to believe, so you don't. What kind of way is that? What d'ya think these people get up on the witness stand for — their health? I'm telling you men the facts are being changed around here. Witnesses are being doubted and there's no reason for it.

5th Juror Witnesses can make mistakes.

10th Juror Sure, when you want 'em to, they do! Know what I mean?

Foreman OK. Let's hold the yelling down.

10th Juror You keep saying that. Maybe what we need is a little yelling in here. These guys are going off every which way. Did hear the scream, didn't hear the scream. What's the difference? They're just little details. You're forgetting the important stuff. I mean, all of a sudden here everybody ...

8th Juror I'd like to call for another vote.

10th Juror Listen, I'm talking here.

Foreman There's another vote called for. How about taking seats?

Jurors who are standing move towards their seats

3rd Juror What are we gonna gain by voting again?

Foreman I don't know. The gentleman asked ...

3rd Juror I never saw so much time spent on nothing.

2nd Juror (*mildly*) It only takes a second.

Foreman OK. I guess the fastest way is to find out who's voting not guilty. All those in favour of "not guilty" raise their hands.

The 5th, 8th and 9th Jurors raise their hands

Still the same. One, two, three "not guiltys". Nine "guiltys".

7th Juror So now where are we? I'm telling you, we can yakety-yak until next Tuesday here. Where's it getting us?

11th Juror Pardon. (*He slowly raises his hand*) I vote "not guilty".

7th Juror Oh, brother!

3rd Juror Oh, now listen! What are you talking about? I mean, we're all going crazy in here or something! This kid is guilty. Why don'tcha pay attention to the facts. (*To the 4th Juror*) Listen, tell him, will ya? This is getting to be a goddamn joke!

Foreman The vote is eight to four, favour of "guilty".

3rd Juror I mean, everybody's heart is starting to bleed for this punk little kid like the President just declared it "Love Your Underprivileged Brother

Week" or something. (*To the 11th Juror*) Listen, I'd like you to tell me why you changed your vote. Come on, give me reasons.

11th Juror I don't have to defend my decision to you. I have a reasonable doubt in my mind.

3rd Juror What reasonable doubt? That's nothing but words. (*He pulls out the switch-knife from the table and holds it up*) Here, look at this. The kid you just decided isn't guilty was seen ramming this thing into his father. Well, look at it, Mr Reasonable Doubt.

9th Juror That's not the knife. Don't you remember?

3rd Juror Brilliant! (*He sticks the knife into the table*)

7th Juror I'm tellin' ya, this is the craziest. (*To the 8th Juror*) I mean, you're sittin' in here pulling stories outa thin air. What're we supposed to believe? (*To the others*) I'm telling you, if this guy was sitting ringside at the Dempsey-Firpo fight, he'd be tryin' to tell us Firpo won. (*To the 8th Juror*) Look, what about the old man? Are we supposed to believe that he didn't get up and run to his door and see the kid tearing down the stairs fifteen seconds after the killing? He's only saying he did to be important. I mean, what's the point of the whole —— ?

5th Juror Hold it a second.

7th Juror And the Milwaukee rooter is heard from.

5th Juror Did the old man say he ran to the door?

7th Juror Ran. Walked. What's the difference? He got there.

6th Juror He said he ran to the door. At least, I think he did.

5th Juror I don't remember what he said. But I don't see how he could run.

4th Juror He said he went from his bedroom to the front door. That's enough, isn't it?

8th Juror Wait a minute. Where was his bedroom, again?

10th Juror Down the hall somewhere. I thought you remembered everything. Don't you remember that?

8th Juror No. Mr Foreman, I'd like to take a look at the diagram of the apartment.

7th Juror Why don't we have them run the trial over just so you can get everything straight?

8th Juror Mr Foreman...

Foreman I heard you.

The Foreman goes to the door and knocks

The Guard unlocks the door and enters

The Foreman confers briefly with him

The Guard exits and locks the door after him

3rd Juror All right, what's this for? How come you're the only one in the room who wants to see exhibits all the time?

5th Juror I want to see this one too.

3rd Juror And I want to stop wasting time.

4th Juror If we're going to start wading through all that business about where the body was found...

8th Juror We're not. Not unless someone else wants to. I'd like to see if a very old man who drags one leg when he walks because he had a stroke last year can get from his bed to his front door in fifteen seconds.

3rd Juror He said twenty seconds.

8th Juror He said fifteen.

3rd Juror Now I'm telling you he said twenty. What're you trying to distort...

11th Juror He said fifteen.

3rd Juror How does he know how long fifteen seconds is? You can't judge that kind of thing.

9th Juror He said fifteen seconds. He was very positive about it.

3rd Juror He's an old man. You saw him. Half the time he was confused. How could he be positive about anything?

The Guard unlocks the door and enters, carrying a large diagram of the apartment

The diagram is a layout of a railroad flat. A bedroom faces the el tracks. Behind it is a series of rooms off a long hall. In the front room is an X marking the spot where the body was found. At the back of the apartment we see the entrance into the apartment hall from the building hall. We see a flight of stairs in the building's hall. Each room is labelled and the dimensions of each room are shown. The Foreman takes the diagram

The Guard exits and locks the door

12th Juror I don't see what we're going to prove here. The man said he saw the boy running out.

8th Juror Well, let's see if the details bear him out. As soon as the body fell to the floor, he said, he heard footsteps upstairs running towards the front door. He heard the upstairs door open and the footsteps start down the stairs. He got to his front door as soon as he could. He swore that it couldn't have been more than fifteen seconds. Now, if the killer began running immediately ——

12th Juror Well, maybe he didn't.

8th Juror The old man said he did.

7th Juror You know, you ought to be down in Atlantic City at that hair-splitters' convention.

6th Juror Listen, baseball, why don't you stop making smart remarks all the time?

7th Juror My friend, for your three dollars a day you've gotta listen to everything.

10th Juror (*to the 8th Juror*) Well, now that you've got that thing in here, what about it?

8th Juror (*to the Foreman*) May I? (*He takes the plan and puts it on a chair*) This is the apartment in which the killing took place. The old man's apartment is directly beneath it and exactly the same. Here are the el tracks. The bedroom. Another bedroom. Bathroom. Living-room. Kitchen. And this is the hall. Here's the front door to the apartment. And here are the stairs. Now, the old man was in bed in this room. (*He indicates the front bedroom*) He says he got up, went out into the hall, down the hall to the front door, opened it and looked out just in time to see the boy racing down the stairs. Am I right so far?

3rd Juror That's the story, for the nineteenth time.

8th Juror Fifteen seconds after he heard the body fall.

11th Juror Correct.

8th Juror His bed was at the window. It's (*he looks closely at the plan*) twelve feet from his bed to the bedroom door. The length of the hall is forty-three feet, six inches. Now he had to get up out of bed, walk twelve feet, open the bedroom door, walk forty-three feet and open the front door — all in fifteen seconds. Do you think he could have done it?

10th Juror Sure he coulda done it.

11th Juror He can only walk very slowly. They had to help him into the witness chair.

3rd Juror You make it sound like a long walk. It's not.

9th Juror For an old man who had a stroke it's a long walk.

The 8th Juror moves his chair and sets the chair to indicate a bed

8th Juror This is the old man's bed.

10th Juror What's going on here?

8th Juror I want to try this thing. Let's see how long it took him.

3rd Juror What d'you mean you want to try it? Why didn't the kid's lawyer bring it up, if it's so important?

5th Juror Well, maybe he just didn't think of it.

10th Juror What d'ya mean, he didn't think of it? You think the man's an idiot or something. It's an obvious thing.

5th Juror Did you think of it?

10th Juror Listen, smart guy. It don't matter whether I thought of it.

Foreman OK, now ... let's hold it down.

10th Juror He didn't bring it up because he knew the answer'd hurt his case. Now what d'ya think of that?

Foreman OK.

8th Juror All right, here's the bed. I'm going to pace off twelve feet, the length of the bedroom. (*He paces twelve feet*)

3rd Juror You're crazy. You can't re-create a thing like that.

11th Juror I'd like to see it.

The 12th Juror picks up his chair and takes it to the 8th Juror. The 8th Juror puts the chair where he is standing

8th Juror All right, this is the bedroom door. The hall is a little over forty-three feet long. I'll pace over to that wall and back again.

The 8th Juror paces counting his steps silently

10th Juror Look, this is absolutely insane. What's the idea of wasting everybody's time here?

8th Juror ... twelve ... (*He stops and turns to the 10th Juror*) According to you it'll only take fifteen seconds. We can spare that. (*He resumes his pacing, counting to himself, and reaches the wall*)

The others watch silently

(*He turns and paces, counting off the rest of the distance*) ... thirty-nine, forty, forty-one, forty-two, forty-three. OK, pass me another chair, please.

The 6th Juror picks up a chair and takes it to the 8th Juror. The 8th Juror places it where he is standing

This is the door to the outside hall and stairway. It was chain-locked according to the testimony. Who's got a watch with a second hand?

2nd Juror I have.

8th Juror When you want me to start, stamp your foot. That'll be the body falling. Time me from there.

The 8th Juror lies down on the two chairs

7th Juror Anyone for charades?

3rd Juror I've never seen anything like this in my whole life!

8th Juror OK. I'm ready.

The 2nd Juror stares at his watch, waiting

10th Juror Come on, let's go here.
2nd Juror I want to wait until the second hand reaches sixty.

They wait. The 2nd Juror suddenly stamps his foot. The 8th Juror rises to a sitting position, swings his legs to the floor and stands up . The 2nd Juror keeps his eyes on his watch. The 8th Juror hobbles, dragging one leg, towards the chair which serves as the bedroom door. He reaches it and pretends to open the door. He then hobbles along the simulated forty-three-foot hallway

10th Juror Come on. Snap it up. He walked twice as fast as that.
11th Juror This is, I think, even more quickly than the old man walked in the courtroom.
8th Juror (*still hobbling*) If you think I should go faster, I will.

The 8th Juror speeds up his pace slightly, reaches the wall, turns and heads for the second chair, the one simulating the door to the outer hallway

3rd Juror Come on, willya! Let's get this kid stuff over with.

They watch as the 8th Juror reaches the last chair. He pretends to open an imaginary chain-lock and then opens the imaginary door

8th Juror Stop!
2nd Juror Right.
8th Juror What's the time?
2nd Juror Fifteen — twenty — thirty — thirty-five — forty — forty-two seconds exactly.
6th Juror Forty-two seconds!
8th Juror I think this is what happened. The old man heard the fight between the boy and his father a few hours earlier. Then, while lying in bed, he heard a body hit the floor in the boy's apartment, and he heard the woman scream from across the street. He got up, tried to get to the door, heard someone racing down the stairs, and assumed it was the boy.
6th Juror I think that's possible.
3rd Juror Assumed? Now listen to me, you people. I've seen all kinds of dishonesty in my day — but this little display takes the cake. You come in here with your sanctimonious talk about slum kids and injustice, and you make up some wild stories, and all of a sudden you start getting through to some of these old ladies in here. Well, you're not getting through to me. I've had enough. What's the matter with you people? Every one of you knows

this kid is guilty. He's got to burn. We're letting him slip through our fingers here.

8th Juror Slip through our fingers? Are you his executioner?

3rd Juror I'm one of 'em.

8th Juror Maybe you'd like to pull the switch.

3rd Juror For this kid? You bet I'd like to pull the switch.

8th Juror I'm sorry for you.

3rd Juror Don't start with me now.

8th Juror Ever since we walked into this room you've been behaving like a self-appointed public avenger.

3rd Juror I'm telling you now! Shut up!

8th Juror You want to see this boy die because you personally want it, not because of the facts.

3rd Juror Shut up!

8th Juror You're a sadist!

3rd Juror Shut up, you son of a bitch!

The 3rd Juror lunges wildly at the 8th Juror

The 8th Juror holds his ground. The 5th and 6th Jurors grab the 3rd Juror from behind. He strains against the hands, his face dark with rage

Let go of me, God damn it! I'll kill him! I'll kill him!

8th Juror (*calmly*) You don't really mean you'll kill me, do you?

The 3rd Juror breaks from the 5th and 6th Jurors, stops struggling and stares bitterly at the 8th Juror as

—— *the* CURTAIN *falls*

ACT II

The same. Immediately following

When the Curtain *rises, the Jurors are in the same positions as they were at the end of the previous Act, looking at the 3rd Juror. There is silence. The 3rd Juror crosses to the window. The other Jurors move about the room. There is an awkward silence*

The Guard unlocks the door and enters

Guard Is there anything wrong, gentlemen? I heard some noise.
Foreman No. There's nothing wrong.

The Foreman collects the apartment plan from the table

Just a little argument. Everything's OK.

The Foreman hands the plan to the Guard

We're finished with this.

The Guard takes the plan, looks carefully around the room, then exits, locking the door behind him

There is a pause. The others look at the 3rd Juror

3rd Juror Well, what are you staring at?

The others, embarrassed, turn away. Some of them take their seats

12th Juror Well — I suppose someone has to — start it off again.
2nd Juror It's getting late. (*To the Foreman*) What do they do, take us out to a restaurant for supper?
Foreman How do I know?
2nd Juror I wonder if they let us go home in case we can't finish tonight. I've got a boy with mumps. He's out to here. The wife says he looks like Khruschev.

The room begins to darken perceptibly now

11th Juror Pardon. This fighting. This is not why we are here, to fight. We have a responsibility. This, I have always thought, is a remarkable thing about democracy. That we are, uh, what is the word? Notified. That we are notified by mail to come down to this place and decide on the guilt or innocence of a man we have never heard of before. We have nothing to gain or lose by our verdict. This is one of the reasons we are strong. We should not make it a personal thing.

12th Juror Um, if no-one else has an idea, I may have a cutie here. I mean, I haven't put much thought into it. Anyway, lemme throw it out on the stoop and see if the cat licks it up.

Foreman See if the cat licks it up? (*He laughs*)

12th Juror Well, it wasn't much of an idea, anyway.

5th Juror Look how dark it's getting. We're gonna have a storm. Boy, it's hot.

The 4th Juror, in tie and jacket, is seemingly not bothered by the heat at all. The 5th Juror turns to him

Pardon me, don't you sweat?

4th Juror No. I don't.

6th Juror Uh, listen, I was wondering if maybe we shouldn't take another vote.

7th Juror Great idea. Maybe we can follow this one up with dancing and refreshments.

6th Juror Mr Foreman?

Foreman It's all right with me. Anyone doesn't want to vote?

No-one answers for a moment

3rd Juror I think we ought to have an open ballot. Call out your votes, y'know. Let's see who stands where.

Foreman That sounds fair. Anyone object? The last vote was eight to four in favour of guilty. All right. I'll call off your jury numbers. I vote "guilty". Number Two?

2nd Juror "Not Guilty."

Foreman Number Three?

3rd Juror "Guilty."

Foreman Number Four?

4th Juror "Guilty."

Foreman Number Five?

5th Juror "Not Guilty."

Foreman Number Six?

6th Juror "Not Guilty."

Foreman Number Seven?

7th Juror "Guilty."

Foreman Number Eight?

8th Juror "Not Guilty."

Foreman Number Nine?

9th Juror "Not Guilty."

Foreman Number Ten?

10th Juror "Guilty."

Foreman Number Eleven?

11th Juror "Not Guilty."

Foreman Number Twelve?

12th Juror "Guilty."

Foreman Six to six.

7th Juror And we go into extra innings here.

10th Juror Six to six! I'm telling you, some of you people in here are out of your minds. A kid like that.

9th Juror I don't think the kind of boy he is has anything to do with it. The facts are supposed to determine the case.

10th Juror Ah, don't give me any of that. I'm sick and tired of facts. You can twist 'em any way you like. Know what I mean?

9th Juror That's exactly the point this gentleman (*he indicates the 8th Juror*) has been making. I mean, you keep shouting at the top of your lungs ...

The 8th Juror puts his hand on the 9th Juror's shoulder. The 9th Juror looks at him and sits

I'd like to be a little younger. (*He stops. Unable to go on*) It's very hot in here.

11th Juror Do you want some water?

9th Juror No, thanks.

It has grown considerably darker in the room and it's oppressively still. There is a murmur of voices at the cooler where the 7th, 10th and 2nd Jurors are in various stages of getting a drink

2nd Juror It's going to rain.

7th Juror No! How did you figure that out, blue eyes? Tell me, how come you switched?

2nd Juror Well, it just seemed to me ——

7th Juror I mean, you haven't got a leg to stand on. You know that, don'tcha?

2nd Juror Well, I don't feel that way. There're a lot of details that never came out.

10th Juror Details! You're just letting yourself get bulldozed by a bunch'a what d'ya call 'em — intellectuals.

2nd Juror Now, that's not so.

10th Juror Ah, come on. You're like everybody else. You think too much, you get mixed up. Know what I mean?

2nd Juror Now, listen, I don't think you have any right to ...

The 10th Juror crosses away

(*Softly*) Loudmouth!

It is now darker than before. There is no movement in the room. Everyone waits for the storm. And suddenly it comes. We hear only the sound of the rain pouring down into the silence. Heads turn towards the window. The rain pours down

The 4th Juror goes into the wash-room and exits to the lavatory

The 8th Juror steps back from the window as the rain splashes in, closes it. The Foreman rises, goes to the light switch at the door and switches on the lights. There is a flickering of harsh white light as the fluorescent lights come on. The rain continues throughout the remainder of the play. The Foreman moves to the 8th Juror

Foreman Wow! Look at that come down, will ya? Think it'll cool things off?

8th Juror Yeah, I guess so.

Foreman Boy! Look at it go! Reminds me of the storm we had — November something. What a storm! Right in the middle of the game.

The 3rd Juror crosses to the wash-room, goes in, switches on the light and washes his hands

We're behind seven-six, but we're just startin' to move the ball, off tackle, y'know. Boom! Boom! Boy, I'll never forget that. We had this kid Slattery. A real ox. Wish I had another one like him. Oh, I probably forgot to tell you — I'm assistant head football coach at the Andrew J. McCorkle High School. That's in Queens.

The 8th Juror smiles briefly

So anyway, we're movin' real nice. Their line is comin' apart. I'm tellin' ya, this Slattery. Boy! And all of a sudden it starts to come down cats and dogs. In two minutes it was mud practically up to your ass. I swear I almost bawled. We couldn't go nowhere.

7th Juror Hey, let's try to get this fan goin' in here. What d'ya say?

The 4th Juror enters the wash-room from the lavatory

The Foreman goes to the bench, stands on it and starts the fan

It musta been connected to the light switch.

The 3rd and 4th Jurors are in the wash-room together

3rd Juror (*to the 4th Juror*) Some rain, huh?

The 4th Juror nods

Well, what d'ya think of this thing? It's even-steven.

The 4th Juror nods

Kind of surprising, isn't it?
4th Juror Yes.
3rd Juror Listen, that business before, you know, where that guy was baiting me. I mean, that doesn't prove anything. Listen, I'm a very excitable person, y'know. So where does he get off to call me a public avenger and a sadist and everything? Anybody in his right mind'd blow his stack, wouldn't he? He was just trying to bait me.
4th Juror He did an excellent job. (*He moves to the towel*) Excuse me. (*He dries his hands*)
3rd Juror OK, maybe he did. I told you, I can't help that kind of thing. I'm a certain type of person, I get moved by this. But let me tell you, I'm sincere.
4th Juror Fine. We all are.

The 10th Juror bursts into the wash-room, strides to the basin and washes his hands

10th Juror Well — isn't this the goddamnedest thing you ever saw? Six to six. It's a joke.
3rd Juror What are we gonna do about it? Can't we break it somehow?
10th Juror Those six bastards in there aren't going to change their minds.
4th Juror Five of them already have changed their minds. There's no reason why they can't be persuaded to do it again.
10th Juror How?
4th Juror Just by using logic.
10th Juror Logic! Holy cow!

3rd Juror Now, just you listen to this man. He's the only one in the room
who knows ...

10th Juror You want my opinion?

4th Juror Go ahead.

10th Juror I think we should just quit.

3rd Juror What the hell are you talking about?

10th Juror Those people in there are suddenly like it's some kind of mission
or something. Look, they're not gonna switch, so let's go and tell the Judge
— we'll be here all night. For Chrissakes, let's tell him we're hung. The
hell with this. I mean, what am I gonna do, break my brains over scum like
that?

3rd Juror Well, that's the most ridiculous thing I ever ... You took an oath
in the courtroom. You can't just quit.

10th Juror Why not?

3rd Juror It's dishonest. Why don't you vote "not guilty"?

10th Juror I voted guilty because I think he's guilty.

3rd Juror But now you don't care what happens?

10th Juror No. Why should I?

4th Juror All right, let's stop this. We're not going to get anywhere like this.

10th Juror Well, what does he want? I gave my honest opinion.

4th Juror I know.

10th Juror I suppose you don't think much of it?

4th Juror No, I don't.

The Foreman opens the wash-room door

Foreman Uh — we'd like to get going in here again, if you don't mind.

The 4th Juror leaves the wash-room

10th Juror (*to the 3rd Juror*) How about him? Is that something?

3rd Juror A hung jury doesn't mean anything. They just have to start the
trial with another jury. That's not what we're here for.

10th Juror What the hell's the difference? A hung jury is what you're gonna
get.

Foreman Look, would you please ...

*The 10th Juror strides out of the wash-room, the 3rd Juror switches out the
light and comes slowly into the room*

10th Juror Listen, I'll tell you what I think. We're goin' nowhere here. I'm
ready to walk into court right now and declare a hung jury.

7th Juror I go for that, too. Let's take it into the Judge and let the kid take his chances with twelve other guys

8th Juror I don't think the court will accept a hung jury. We haven't been in here very long.

7th Juror Well, let's find out.

11th Juror I'm not in favour of this.

7th Juror (*to the 11th Juror*) Listen, this kid wouldn't stand a chance with another jury and you know it. (*To the others*) Come on, we're hung. Nobody's gonna change his opinion. Let's take it inside.

5th Juror You still don't think there's any room for reasonable doubt?

7th Juror No, I don't.

11th Juror Pardon. Maybe you don't fully understand the term "reasonable doubt".

7th Juror What d'ya mean, I don't understand it? Who the hell are you to talk to me like that? (*To the others*) How d'ya like this guy? I'm tellin' ya they're all alike. He comes over to this country running for his life and before he can even take a big breath he's telling us how to run the show. The arrogance of the guy!

5th Juror (*to the 7th Juror*) You mean you're calling him arrogant because he wasn't born here? Well, I'm calling you arrogant because you were. How's that?

11th Juror Please, please. It doesn't matter.

7th Juror Look, sonny, nobody around here's gonna tell me what words I understand and what words I don't. (*He points to the 11th Juror*) Especially him. Because I'll knock his goddamn Middle European head off.

Foreman All right. Let's stop arguing for two minutes in here. Can't we stick to the subject?

8th Juror I'd like to go over something, if you gentlemen don't mind. An important point for the prosecution was the fact that the boy, after he claimed he was at the movies during the hours the killing took place, couldn't name the pictures he saw or the stars who appeared in them. (*He points to the 4th Juror*) This gentleman has repeated that point in here several times.

4th Juror That's correct. It was the only alibi the boy offered and he himself couldn't back it up with any details at all.

8th Juror Putting yourself in the boy's place, if you can, do you think you'd be able to remember details after an upsetting experience such as being struck in the face by your father?

4th Juror I think so, if there were any special details to remember. He couldn't remember the movies at the theatre he named because he wasn't there that night.

8th Juror According to the police testimony in court he was questioned by the police in the kitchen of his apartment while the body of his father was lying on the floor in the bedroom. Do you think you could remember details under such circumstances.

4th Juror I do.

8th Juror Under great emotional stress?

4th Juror Under great emotional stress.

8th Juror He remembered the movies in court. He named them correctly and he named the stars who played in them.

4th Juror Yes, his lawyer took great pains to bring that out. He had three months from the night of the murder to the day of the trial in which to memorize them. I'll take the testimony of the policeman who interrogated him right after the murder, when he couldn't remember a thing about the movies, great emotional stress or not.

8th Juror I'd like to ask you a personal question.

4th Juror Go ahead.

8th Juror Where were you last night?

4th Juror I was home.

8th Juror What about the night before last?

10th Juror Come on, what is this?

4th Juror (*to the 10th Juror*) It's perfectly all right. (*To the 8th Juror*) I went from court to my office and stayed there till eight thirty. Then I went straight home to bed.

8th Juror And the night before that?

4th Juror That was — Tuesday. I — was — oh, yes. That was the night of the bridge tournament. I played bridge.

8th Juror And Monday night.

7th Juror When you get him down to New Year's Eve, nineteen fifty lemme know.

4th Juror (*trying to remember*) Monday. (*He pauses*) Monday night. (*He remembers*) Monday night my wife and I went to the movies.

8th Juror What did you see?

4th Juror *The Scarlet Circle*. It's a very clever whodunit.

8th Juror What was the second feature?

4th Juror (*straining*) *The* ... I'll tell you in a minute. *The* — *Remarkable Mrs Something*. Mrs — uh — Mainbridge. No, Bainbridge. *The Remarkable Mrs Bainbridge*.

2nd Juror Excuse me. I saw that. It's called *The Amazing Mrs Bainbridge*.

4th Juror *The* — *Amazing Mrs Bainbridge*. Yes. I think that's right.

8th Juror Who was in *The Amazing Mrs Bainbridge*?

4th Juror Barbara — Long, I think. She's a dark, very pretty girl. Barbara — Lang — Lane — something like that.

8th Juror Who else?

The 4th Juror takes a handkerchief and mops his suddenly sweating forehead

4th Juror Well, I'd never heard of them before. It was a very inexpensive second feature, with unknown ...

8th Juror And you weren't under an emotional strain, were you?

4th Juror No, I wasn't.

9th Juror I think the point is made.

10th Juror Big point!

9th Juror I think it is a big point.

10th Juror What? Just because he can't remember the name of some two-bit movie star? I suppose that proves the kid was at the movies.

9th Juror No. But it indicates that no-one can prove he wasn't. He might have been at the movies and forgotten what he saw. It's possible. If it's perfectly normal for this gentleman (*he indicates the 4th Juror*) — to forget a few details, then it's also perfectly normal for the boy. Being accused of murder isn't necessarily supposed to give him an infallible memory.

10th Juror (*to the 9th Juror*) You can talk till your tongue is draggin' on the floor. The boy is guilty. Period. Know what I mean, my friend? Who's got those cough drops?

2nd Juror They're all gone, my friend.

Foreman Y'know, there's something we're forgetting here that I was just thinking about. That whole business with the psychiatrist that dragged on forever.

10th Juror Now don't start with all that phoney psycho-what-ever-you-call-it-stuff. What a racket that is! Filling people's heads with all that junk. Listen, I've got three psychiatrists keeping their cars in one of my garages. The whole three of 'em are crazy.

Foreman Listen, there's a point I'm tryin' to make here. Do you mind?

10th Juror I wouldn't give you a nickel for a psychiatrist's testimony.

8th Juror Why don't you let the man talk? You can take five minutes on the uselessness of psychiatry when he's finished.

Foreman What I was gonna say was, the psychiatrist definitely stated that the boy had strong homicidal tendencies. I mean, that he was, what d'ya call it — capable of committing murder. He described all those tests, inkblots and all that stuff, and he said the kid is definitely a killer-type. Am I right?

12th Juror Check. I think he said something about paranoid tendencies if I'm not mistaken.

Foreman Right. Whatever that is, he said it. Let's not forget, we're talking about a boy who always had murder on his mind.

12th Juror His unconscious mind.

Foreman Nobody else's.

11th Juror I beg pardon, in discussing ——

10th Juror I beg pardon. What are you so goddamn polite about?

11th Juror For the same reason you're not. It's the way I was brought up.

(*He turns to the others*) In discussing such a thing as the murder potential we should remember that many of us are capable of committing murder. But few of us do. We impose controls upon ourselves to prevent it. The most these psychiatric tests can accomplish along these lines is this: they can tell us that some day a particular person may commit a murder. That's all. They prove nothing.

4th Juror Then how come they're admitted in evidence?

11th Juror They have many uses, of course. In this case they added to the general impression the prosecution was trying to create. Perhaps we would find that if we twelve men took the same tests, one or two of us might be discovered to have unconscious desires to kill, and the potentiality of carrying them out. Yet none of us has. To say that a man is capable of murder does not mean that he has committed murder.

10th Juror But it can mean it. Listen, if they said the kid is capable of killing, he could've killed couldn't he?

8th Juror You're the one who said, and I quote, "I wouldn't give you a nickel for a psychiatrist's testimony."

10th Juror Boy, I'm telling you ... (*He crosses to the 8th Juror*) I'd like to ... (*He stops*)

The 8th Juror does not look up at him. The 10th Juror crosses angrily away

6th Juror What time is it?

7th Juror It's five of six. Man, look at that rain.

12th Juror There goes your ball game.

2nd Juror (*to the 8th Juror*) Say, could I see that knife for a second?

The 8th Juror slides the knife across the table to the 2nd Juror who opens and examines it

Foreman Well, we're still tied up six to six. Who's got a suggestion?

12th Juror I have. Let's get some dinner.

5th Juror Why don't we wait till seven? Give it another hour.

12th Juror OK with me.

2nd Juror Um — there's something I'd like to say. I mean, it's been bothering me a little and as long as we're stuck ... Well, there was this whole business about the stab wound and how it was made, the downward angle of it, you know?

3rd Juror Don't tell me we're gonna start with that. They went over it and over it.

2nd Juror I know they did, but I don't go along with it. The boy is five feet, seven inches tall. His father was six two. That's a difference of seven inches. It's a very awkward thing to stab down into the chest of someone who 's more than a half a foot taller than you are.

3rd Juror (*crossing to the 2nd Juror and indicating the knife*) Give me that.

The 2nd Juror hands the knife to the 3rd Juror

Look, you're not gonna be satisfied till you see it again. I'm gonna give you a demonstration. Somebody get up.

There is a pause. No-one moves for a moment, and then the 8th Juror rises and crosses to the 3rd Juror. They stand looking at each other

OK. (*To the 2nd Juror*) Now, watch this. I don't want to have to do it again. (*He turns to the 8th Juror, looks squarely at him, and squats to make himself shorter*) I'm six or seven inches shorter than you. Right?

2nd Juror That's right. Maybe a little more.

3rd Juror OK. Let it be more.

The 3rd Juror flicks open the knife, changes its position in his hand and holds it aloft, ready to stab downwards

The 8th Juror and the 3rd Juror look steadily at each other, then the 3rd Juror suddenly stabs downward, hard

2nd Juror Look out!

The blade stops about an inch from the 8th Juror's chest. The 8th Juror does not move. The 3rd Juror smiles

6th Juror That's not funny.

5th Juror What's the matter with you?

3rd Juror Now just calm down. Nobody's hurt. Right?

8th Juror No. Nobody's hurt.

3rd Juror All right. There's your angle. Take a look at it. Down and in. That's how I'd stab a taller man in the chest and that's how it was done. Now go ahead and tell me I'm wrong.

The 3rd Juror hands the knife to the 8th Juror and crosses away. The 12th Juror crosses to the 8th Juror and using his closed hand, simulates stabbing the 8th Juror in the chest

12th Juror Down and in. I guess there's no argument.

5th Juror (*moving to the 8th Juror*) Wait a minute. Give me that.

The 8th Juror hands the knife to the 5th Juror. He closes the knife and holds it gingerly

I hate these things. I grew up with them.

8th Juror Have you seen them used in fights?

5th Juror Too many of them. On my stoop. In my backyard. In the lot across the street. Switch-knives came with the neighbourhood where I lived. Funny, I wasn't thinking of it. I guess you try to forget those things. You don't use this kind of knife that way. You have to hold it like this to release the blade. In order to stab downwards, you would have to change your grip.

8th Juror How do you use it?

5th Juror Underhanded.

The 5th Juror flicks the knife open and, holding it underhanded, swings round and slashes swiftly forward and upward

Like that. Anyone who's ever used a switch-knife'd never handle it any other way.

8th Juror Are you sure?

5th Juror I'm sure.

The 5th Juror closes the blade and flicks it open again

That's why they're made like this.

8th Juror Everyone agreed that the boy is pretty handy with a knife, didn't they?

5th Juror That's right.

8th Juror (*to the 5th Juror*) Do you think he would have made the kind of wound that killed his father?

5th Juror Not with the experience he'd had with these things. No, I don't think he would. He'd go for him underhanded ...

3rd Juror How do you know? What — were you in the room when the father was killed?

5th Juror No, and neither was anyone else.

The 5th Juror sticks the knife in the table and crosses away

3rd Juror (*to the 8th Juror*) You're giving us a lot of mumbo-jumbo here. I don't believe it.

4th Juror I don't think you can determine what type of wound this boy might or might not have made simply because he knows how to handle a knife.

3rd Juror That's right. That's absolutely right.

8th Juror (*looking at the 12th Juror*) What do you think?

The 12th Juror hesitates for a moment. He is confused, but trying to be honest

12th Juror Well — I don't know ...
3rd Juror What d'ya mean — you don't know?
12th Juror I don't know.
8th Juror (*to the 7th Juror*) What about you?

The 7th Juror looks around the table momentarily

4th Juror Just a minute. According to the woman across the street ...
7th Juror Listen, I'll tell you something. I'm a little sick of this whole thing already. All this yakkin's gettin' us nowhere so I'm going to break it up here. I'm changing my vote to "not guilty".
3rd Juror You're what?
7th Juror You heard me. I've had enough.
3rd Juror What d'you mean — you've had enough? That's no answer.
7th Juror Hey, listen you! Just worry about yourself!
11th Juror (*crossing to the 7th Juror*) He's right. That is not an answer. What kind of man are you? You have sat here and voted guilty with everyone else because there are some baseball tickets burning a hole in your pocket. Now you have changed your vote because you say you're sick of all the talking here.
7th Juror Listen. buddy ——
11th Juror You have no right to play like this with a man's life. This is a terrible and ugly thing to do. Don't you care ... ?
7th Juror Now, wait a minute. You can't talk like that to me!
11th Juror I can talk like that to you. If you want to vote not guilty, then do it because you're convinced the man is not guilty — not because you've had enough. And if you think he's guilty, then vote that way, or don't you have the guts to do what you think is right?
7th Juror Now, listen ...
11th Juror Guilty or not guilty?
7th Juror I told you — not guilty.
11th Juror Why?
7th Juror God damn you. I don't have to ——
11th Juror You do have to. Say it. Why?
7th Juror (*in a low voice*) I — don't think he's guilty.

The 11th Juror looks disgustedly at the 7th Juror then moves to his chair. The 7th Juror stands defeated

8th Juror Mr Foreman, I want another vote.
Foreman OK, there's another vote called for.

The Jurors cross to their chairs and sit

I guess the quickest way is a show of hands. Anybody object?

There is no answer

All those voting "not guilty" raise your hands.

The 2nd, 5th, 6th, 7th, 8th, 9th and 11th Jurors raise their hands immediately

One. Two. Three. Four. Five. Six. Seven.

The 12th Juror's face is a mask of indecision, then he suddenly raises his hand

Eight.

The Foreman stops counting and looks around the table. Slowly, almost embarrassed, he raises his own hand

Nine. (*He lowers his hand*) All those voting "guilty".

The 3rd, 4th and 10th Jurors raise their hands

Nine to three in favour of "not guilty".

10th Juror I don't understand you people. I mean, all these picky little points you keep bringing up. They don't mean nothing. How can you believe his story? (*To the 11th Juror*) You're an intelligent man. Well, you're not gonna tell me you're not. You know the facts of life. Well, for Chrissakes look at what we're dealing with here. You know what they're like! I mean, that guy (*he points to the 8th Juror*) — over there, well, I don't know what the hell is going on with him. All that talk about psychiatrists. Maybe he oughta go to one. Look, let's talk facts. These people are born to lie. Now, it's the way they are and no intelligent man is gonna tell me otherwise. They don't know what the truth is. Well, take a look at them. They are different. They think different. They act different. Well, for instance, they don't need any big excuse to kill someone.

The 5th Juror crosses to the wash-room door

Well, that's true. Everybody knows it. They get drunk on wine or something cheap like that. Oh, they're very big drinkers.

The 5th Juror goes into the wash-room, slams the door behind him

Smart guy! Look at him for Chrissakes! What does that mean, slamming
the door? And then they're drunk, and all of a sudden — bang —
somebody's lying dead in the gutter. OK, nobody's blaming them for it.
That's how they are, by nature, y'know what I mean? Violent! Human life
don't mean as much to them as it does to us.

*The 11th Juror rises and crosses to the wash-room door. He follows the 5th
Juror*

Where are you going?

The 11th Juror does not reply and goes into the wash-room

While you're in there, clean out your ears, maybe you'll hear something.

The 4th Juror rises and moves to the window

Look, you listen to me now. These people are boozing it up, and fighting
all the time, and if somebody gets killed, so somebody gets killed. They
don't care. Family don't mean anything to them. They breed like animals.
Fathers, mothers, that don't mean anything. Oh sure, there are some good
things about 'em. Look, I'm the first one to say that. I've known some who
were OK, but that's the exception.
9th Juror Do you know you're a sick man?
10th Juror Sick?
9th Juror Why don't you sit down?
10th Juror You old son of a bitch! Who the hell are you?

The 6th Juror moves towards the 9th Juror

The 12th Juror steps between the 9th and 10th Jurors

(*To the 12th Juror*) No. Who the hell is he to tell me that? Sick. Look at him
— he can hardly stand up. Listen, I'm speaking my piece here and you're
gonna listen.

The 9th Juror moves to the window

12th Juror Maybe if you just quieted down.
10th Juror I will like hell quiet down. There is not one of them, not one who's
any good. Now, d'you hear that? Not one. Now let me lay this out for you
— ignorant — bastards. (*To the 9th Juror*) You at the window, you're so
goddamned smart. We're facing a danger here. Don't you know it? These

people are multiplying. That kid on trial, his type, they're multiplying five times as fast as we are. That's the statistic. Five times. And they are — wild animals. They're against us, they hate us, they want to destroy us. That's right. (*To the 6th Juror*) Don't look at me like that! There's a danger. For God's sake, we're living in a dangerous time, and if we don't watch it, if we don't smack them down whenever we can, then they are gonna own us. They're gonna breed us out of existence.

6th Juror Ah, shut up!

10th Juror Now you goddamned geniuses had better listen to me. They're violent, they're vicious, they're ignorant, and they will cut us up. That's their intent. To cut us up. (*To the 7th Juror*) I'm warning you. This boy, this boy on trial here. We've got him. That's one at least. I say get him before his kind gets us. I don't give a goddamn about the law. Why should I? They don't. Now I'm telling you.

2nd Juror I've heard enough. Now you just stop all this.

10th Juror (*looking angrily at the 2nd Juror*) How would you like me to cave your head in for you, you smart little bastard? Where the hell do you get the gall ... ?

The 4th Juror steps in front of the 10th Juror and stops him firmly

4th Juror We've heard enough. Sit down. And don't open your filthy mouth again.

The 4th and 10th Jurors stare at each other. Finally, the 10th Juror turns away, crosses to a chair and sits with his back to the others. The other Jurors (including the 5th and 11th Jurors) slowly cross to their seats

8th Juror It's very hard to keep personal prejudice out of a thing like this. And no matter where you run into it, prejudice obscures the truth. Well, I don't think any real damage has been done here. Because I don't really know what the truth is. No-one ever will, I suppose. Nine of us now seem to feel that the defendant is innocent, but we're just gambling on probabilities. We may be wrong. We may be trying to return a guilty man to the community. No-one can really know. But we have a reasonable doubt, and this is a safeguard which has enormous value in our system. No jury can declare a man guilty unless it's sure. We nine can't understand how you three are still so sure. Maybe you can tell us.

4th Juror I'll try. You've made some excellent points. The last one, in which you argued that the boy wouldn't have made the kind of overhand stab wound that killed his father, was very persuasive. But I still believe the boy is guilty of murder. I have two reasons. One: the evidence given by the woman across the street who actually saw the murder committed.

3rd Juror And how, brother! As far as I'm concerned that's the most important testimony in the whole case.

4th Juror And two: the fact that this woman described the stabbing by saying she saw the boy raise his arm over his head and plunge the knife down into his father's chest. She saw him do it — the wrong way.

3rd Juror That's right! That's absolutely right!

4th Juror Now, let's talk about this woman for a minute. She said that she went to bed at about eleven o'clock that night. Her bed was next to the window — and she could look out while lying down and see directly into the boy's window across the tracks. She tossed and turned for over an hour, unable to fall asleep. Finally, she turned towards the window at about ten minutes after twelve, and, as she looked out, she saw the killing through the windows of the passing el train. She says that the lights went out immediately after the killing but that she got a good look at the boy in the act of stabbing his father. As far as I can see, this is unshakeable testimony.

3rd Juror That's what I mean. That's the whole case.

4th Juror (*to the 8th Juror*) What do you think?

The 8th Juror remains silent

(*Looking at the 12th Juror*) How about you?

12th Juror Well — I don't know. There's so much evidence to sift. This is a pretty complicated business.

4th Juror Frankly, I don't see how we can vote for acquittal.

12th Juror Well, it's not so easy to arrange the evidence in order.

3rd Juror You can throw out all the other evidence. The woman saw him do it. What else do you want?

12th Juror Well, maybe ...

3rd Juror Let's vote on it.

Foreman OK. There's another vote called for. Anybody object?

12th Juror I'm changing my vote. I think he's "guilty".

3rd Juror Anybody else? The vote is eight to four.

11th Juror (*to the 3rd Juror*) What makes you consider this one vote a personal triumph?

3rd Juror I'm the competitive type. (*To the others*) OK. Now here's what I think. I think we're a hung jury. Let's take it inside to the Judge.

4th Juror You didn't want a hung jury before.

3rd Juror Well, I want it now.

4th Juror I don't understand that. You thought it was immoral to ——

3rd Juror I don't any more. There are people in here who are so goddamned stubborn that you can't even ... We'll never get this thing done. We'll be here for a week. Well, I want to hear an argument. I say we're a hung jury.

(*He turns to the 8th Juror*) Come on. You're the leader of the cause. What about it?

8th Juror Let's go over it again.

3rd Juror We went over it again. (*He waves towards the 12th Juror*) J. Walter Thompson over there is bouncing backwards and forwards like a tennis ball ...

12th Juror Wait a second. You have no right to ...

The 4th Juror removes his spectacles and polishes them

3rd Juror I apologize on my knees. (*To the 8th Juror*) Come on. Let's get out from under this thing.

4th Juror All right. Maybe we can talk about setting some kind of a time limit. (*Still polishing his spectacles, he turns and peers up at the clock*) The time is ... (*He squints and puts on his spectacles*)

3rd Juror Quarter after six.

4th Juror (*looking at the clock*) Quarter after six. (*He removes his spectacles and lays them on the table. He looks tired. He closes his eyes and clasps his fingers over the marks left by his spectacles at the sides of his nose. He rubs these areas as he speaks*) Someone before mentioned seven o'clock. I think that's a point at which we might begin to discuss the question of whether we're a hung jury or not.

The 9th Juror looks closely at the 4th Juror and obviously has thought of something tremendously exciting

9th Juror (*to the 4th Juror*) Don't you feel well?

4th Juror I feel perfectly well — thank you. (*To the others*) I was saying that seven o'clock would be a reasonable time to ——

9th Juror The reason I asked about that was because you were rubbing your nose like ... I'm sorry for interrupting. But you made a gesture that reminded me ——

4th Juror I'm trying to settle something here. Do you mind?

9th Juror I think this is important.

4th Juror Very well.

9th Juror Thank you. I'm sure you'll pardon me for this, but I was wondering why you were rubbing your nose like that?

3rd Juror Ah, come on, now, will ya please!

9th Juror Right now I happen to be talking to this gentleman here. (*To the 4th Juror*) Now, why were you rubbing your nose?

4th Juror Well, if it's any of your business, I was rubbing it because it bothers me a little.

9th Juror I'm sorry. Is it because of your eyeglasses?

4th Juror It is. Now could we get on to something else?

9th Juror Your eyeglasses make those deep impressions on the sides of your nose. I hadn't noticed that before. They must be annoying.

4th Juror They are very annoying.

9th Juror I wouldn't know about that. I've never worn eyeglasses. (*He points to his eyes and smiles*) Twenty-twenty.

7th Juror Listen, will you come on already with the optometrist bit.

9th Juror (*to the 4th Juror*) The woman who testified that she saw the killing had these same deep marks on the sides of her nose.

8th Juror That's right, she did.

There is a silence in the room and then a babble of ad lib conversation

9th Juror Please. Just a minute and then I'll be finished. I don't know if anyone else noticed that about her. I didn't think about it then but I've been going over her face in my mind. She had those marks. She kept rubbing them in court.

5th Juror He's right. She did do that a lot.

9th Juror This woman was about forty-five years old. She was making a tremendous effort to look thirty-five for her first public appearance. Heavy make-up. Dyed hair. Brand-new clothes that should have been worn by a younger woman. No eyeglasses. See if you can get a mental picture of her.

3rd Juror What d'ya mean, no glasses? You don't know if she wore glasses. Just because she was rubbing her nose ...

5th Juror She has those marks. I saw 'em.

3rd Juror So what? What d'ya think that means?

Foreman Listen, I saw 'em, too. He's right. I was the closest one to her. She had these deep things, what d'ya call 'em, uh — you know.

The Foreman massages the spot on his nose where they should be

3rd Juror Well, what point are you making here?

Foreman She had those marks.

3rd Juror She had dyed hair and marks on her nose. I'm asking ya what does that mean?

9th Juror Could those marks be made by anything other than eyeglasses?

4th Juror No. They couldn't.

3rd Juror (*to the 4th Juror*) Listen, what are you saying here? I didn't see any marks.

4th Juror I did. Strange, but I didn't think about it before.

3rd Juror Well, what about the lawyer? Why didn't he say anything?

8th Juror There are twelve people in here concentrating on this case. Eleven of us didn't think of it, either.

3rd Juror OK, Clarence Darrow. Then what about the District Attorney? You think he'd try to pull a trick like that, have her testify without glasses?

8th Juror Did you ever see a woman who had to wear glasses and didn't want to because she thinks they spoil her looks?

6th Juror My wife. Listen, I'm telling ya, as soon as we walk outa the house ...

8th Juror Maybe the District Attorney didn't know, either.

6th Juror Yeah, that's what I was just gonna say.

3rd Juror OK. She had marks on her nose. I'm givin' ya this. From glasses. Right? She never wore 'em out of the house so people'd think she was gorgeous. But when she saw this kid kill his father she was in the house. Alone. That's all.

8th Juror (*to the 4th Juror*) Do you wear your eyeglasses when you go to bed?

4th Juror No, I don't. No-one wears eyeglasses to bed.

8th Juror It's logical to say that she wasn't wearing them while she was in bed, tossing and turning, trying to fall asleep.

3rd Juror How do you know?

8th Juror I don't know. I'm guessing. I'm also guessing that she probably didn't put on her glasses when she turned and looked casually out of the window. And she herself said that the murder took place just as she looked out and the lights went off a split second later. She couldn't have had time to put glasses on then.

3rd Juror Wait a second ...

8th Juror And here's another guess. Maybe she honestly thought she saw the boy kill his father. I say that she saw only a blur.

3rd Juror How do you know what she saw? How does he know all these things? (*To the 8th Juror*) You don't know what kind of glasses she wore. Maybe she was farsighted. Maybe they were sunglasses. What do you know about it?

8th Juror I only know that the woman's eyesight is in question now.

11th Juror She had to identify a person sixty feet away in the dark, without glasses.

2nd Juror You can't send someone off to die on evidence like that.

3rd Juror Don't give me that!

8th Juror Don't you think that the woman might have made a mistake?

3rd Juror No!

8th Juror It's not possible?

3rd Juror No! It's not possible.

8th Juror (*to the 12th Juror*) Is it possible?

12th Juror Yes. I say "not guilty".

8th Juror (*to the 10th Juror*) Do you still think he's guilty?

10th Juror Yes, I think he's guilty. But I couldn't care less. You smart bastards do whatever you want to do.

8th Juror How do you vote?

10th Juror "Not guilty." Do whatever you want.

3rd Juror You're the worst son a ... I think he's guilty.

8th Juror Does anyone else think he's guilty?

4th Juror No, I'm convinced.

3rd Juror What's the matter with you?

4th Juror I now have a reasonable doubt.

9th Juror It's eleven to one.

3rd Juror Well, what about all the other evidence? What about all that stuff — the knife — the whole business?

2rd Juror You said we could throw out all the other evidence.

8th Juror (*to the 3rd Juror*) You're alone.

3rd Juror I don't care whether I'm alone or not. It's my right.

8th Juror It's your right.

3rd Juror Well, what d'ya want? I say he's guilty.

8th Juror We want your arguments.

3rd Juror I gave you my arguments.

8th Juror We're not convinced. We want to hear them again. We have as much time as it takes.

3rd Juror Everything — every single thing that came out in that courtroom, but I mean everything, says he's guilty. Do you think I'm an idiot or something? You lousy bunch of bleeding hearts. You're not goin' to intimidate me. I'm entitled to my opinion. I can sit in this goddamn room for a year. Somebody say something.

The others watch silently

Why don'tcha take that stuff about the old man — the old man who lived there — and heard everything. Or take the knife, what — just because he — found one like it? The old man saw him. Right there on the stairs. What's the difference how many seconds it took? What's the difference? Every single thing. The knife falling through a hole in his pocket — you can't prove that he didn't get to the door. Sure you can hobble around the room all you want, but you can't prove it. I'm telling you every single thing that went on has been twisted and turned in here. That business with the glasses, how do you know she didn't have them on? The woman testified in court. Well, what d'ya want? That's it.

The others are silent

That's the whole case.

The others are silent

That whole thing about hearing the boy yell? The phrase was "I'm gonna
kill you." That's what he said. To his own father. I don't care what kind of
man that was. It was his father. That goddamn rotten kid. I know him. What
they're like. What they do to you. How they kill you every day. My God,
don't you see? How come I'm the only one who sees? Jeez, I can feel that
knife goin' in.
8th Juror It's not your boy. He's somebody else.
4th Juror Let him live.

There's a long pause

3rd Juror All right. "Not guilty".

The Foreman moves to the door and knocks on it

The Guard unlocks the door and enters

Foreman We have a verdict.
Guard All right, gentlemen. Take your seats in the jury box.

The Guard exits

*The Foreman and the other jurors collect their jackets, etc., and all except
the 3rd and the 8th Jurors follow him off*

*The 3rd Juror remains seated. Finally only he and the 8th Juror remain in
the room. The 8th Juror puts on his own jacket and brings the 3rd Juror's
jacket to him. The 3rd Juror rises. The 8th Juror helps him on with his jacket*

The 3rd Juror exits

*The 8th Juror follows, but pauses at the door and looks back at the empty
jury-room. The knife still sticks into the table. The 8th Juror exits. The rain
has stopped*

Curtain

Page 24 — Tic-tac-toe is noughts and crosses

FURNITURE AND PROPERTY LIST

On stage: Door with practical lock
Table. *On it:* pencils, notepads, ashtrays
Twelve chairs
Extra chairs (one by the window)
Small table
Water-cooler with paper cups. *Over it:* clock
Bench. *Over it:* electric fan (practical)
Waste-basket
Coat-hooks. *Over them:* shelf
Windows. *To open* Act I: windows closed. *To open* Act II: windows open
In wash-room: wash-basin, soap container, towels

Off stage: Clipboard with list and pen, doorkey (**Guard**)
Switch-knife with tag (**Guard**)
Plan of apartment (**Guard**)

Personal: **Foreman:** watch
2nd Juror: watch, package of cough drops
3rd Juror: notes
4th Juror: newspaper, eyeglasses, tie, handkerchief
7th Juror: watch, chewing gum, handkerchief
8th Juror: switch-knife
10th Juror: handkerchief

LIGHTING PLOT

Practical fittings required: fluorescent lighting in jury-room with light-switch by the door

ACT I

To open: Effect of sunlight. Wash-room light on

Cue 1   **8th Juror** switches off the wash-room light   (Page 22)
            Snap off wash-room light

ACT II

To open: Lights as at end of previous Act

Cue 2   **2nd Juror**: "... looks like Khruschev."   (Page 38)
            Commence slow dim of general lighting for effect
            of gathering storm

Cue 3   **Foreman** switches on the lights   (Page 41)
            Snap on practical with fluorescent flicker effect

Cue 4   **3rd Juror** switches on the wash-room light   (Page 41)
            Snap on wash-room lighting

Cue 5   **3rd Juror** switches off the wash-room light   (Page 43)
            Snap off wash-room lightimg

EFFECTS PLOT

ACT I

No Cues

ACT II

Cue 1   **2nd Juror:** "Loudmouth!"   (Page 41)
            Commence rain effect

The rain continues throughout the remainder of the play with occasional thunder and flashes of lightning

Cue 2   **8th Juror** exits   (Page 59)
            The rain stops

PRINTED IN GREAT BRITAIN BY
THE LONGDUNN PRESS LTD., BRISTOL.